Foreword by TIM SANDERS
Author of the *New York Times* bestseller *Love Is the Killer App*

ESSENTIAL
ACCOUNT
PLANNING

**5 KEYS FOR HELPING YOUR SALES TEAM
DRIVE REVENUE**

MARK DONNOLO

ATD Press is an internationally renowned source of insightful and practical information on talent development, workplace learning, and professional development.

ATD Press
1640 King Street
Alexandria, VA 22314 USA

Ordering information: Books published by ATD Press can be purchased by visiting ATD's website at www.td.org/books or by calling 800.628.2783 or 703.683.8100.

Library of Congress Control Number: 2017936839
ISBN-10: 1-56286-776-8
ISBN-13: 978-1-56286-776-8
e-ISBN: 978-1-56286-777-5

ATD Press Editorial Staff
Director: Kristine Luecker
Manager: Melissa Jones
Community of Practice Manager, Sales Enablement: Roxy Torres
Developmental Editor: Jack Harlow
Senior Associate Editor: Caroline Coppel
Cover Design: Faceout Studio, Tim Green
Text Design: Francelyn Fernandez
Printed by Data Reproductions Corporation, Auburn Hills, MI

Contents

Foreword

I first encountered Mark Donnolo's work when I read his book *The Innovative Sale.* I was impressed with how he applied a step-by-step approach to thinking creatively as a sales professional. His observations about the link between teamwork and sales innovation resonated with my experiences as a practitioner and consultant. When he approached me recently about reviewing his new work, I leapt at the opportunity, and later agreed to write this foreword.

Essential Account Planning: 5 Keys for Helping Your Sales Team Drive Revenue is an important book for sales leaders and contributors because more than ever, strategic accounts are critical to enterprise success and harder than ever to win and keep.

Your most strategic accounts are your marketing department's best friend when it comes to building a brand as a trusted winner in your market. With so many cloud and niche companies eating away at the midsized and smallest accounts in your market, only the strategic ones serve as a barrier to entry. Moreover, strategic accounts offer your enterprise a volume of transactions, challenges, and insights that enable you to stay one step ahead of your market.

Ten years ago, your strategic account likely had a decision maker or two, in a situation where you sold belly-to-belly against a handful of competitors. Today, the game has changed significantly, as your average high-quality sale involves six or more decision makers, end users, sign-offs, and influencers—many of which you'll never get face time with! Globalization, cloud computing, and crowd-sourcing have created a highly competitive marketplace in which any strategic account can be lured away by a hungry startup looking to work cheap or for free to "win more logos."

In this book, you'll discover five imperatives, or strategies, that will help you cut through the rising complexity of the sale, win the account, and keep it—growing it year over year. It's likely that your current sales methodology was not created with the strategic account in mind, opting instead to "average out" the account mix so the funnel works right at any sales level. Few if any methodologies possess a detailed plan that treats strategic accounts like the unique animals they are. To paraphrase a chief sales officer at a major computer-hardware maker, "When it comes to your most critical accounts, without a process, you get a mess."

I'm not just a fellow author; I'm also a business-book reader, just like you. I buy books like this one because I want to be on top of my game and solve sales challenges. The best way to approach reading *Essential Account Planning* is to put yourself inside the many great stories shared in the coming pages. Note how the challenges and organizational issues described are similar to yours. After you finish the book, locate at least three situations where you can apply the imperatives immediately. Use the templates in the appendices as your tools; they will be very helpful in implementation.

Share what you learn with your team and challenge them to think about the existing strategic account planning process (if there is one) and how important it is to master. If you want to make the leap from contributor to sales leader, driving a winning process that moves the needle is a good path to success. If you are a sales leader who wants your team to win in the market consistently and grow in their professional skill set, invest the time to learn and then share Mark's elegant framework for strategic account management.

There's an underlying perspective to *Essential Account Planning* that offers you a chance to dramatically boost your sales performance: Strategic account management is a team sport. Unlike transactional accounts, which buy off-the-shelf products or services based on price, convenience, and reliability, most strategic accounts require customization and compromise. This means that sales must work across departmental lines, with strategic account managers serving the role of quarterback, marshaling political and organizational resources to satisfy the demands of high-value clients.

I believe too many people practice fake strategic account planning these days. They confuse activity management, forecasting, and service-plan review with the type of defined process this book lays out. To them, I quote my old friend, quality guru W. Edward Deming: "If you can't describe what you are doing as a process, you don't know what you are doing."

Tim Sanders, Former Chief Sales Officer at Yahoo!
Author of *Dealstorming: The Secret Weapon That Can Solve
Your Toughest Sales Challenges*

Introduction

I sat across the table from the head of sales for a multinational manufacturing company. The end of Q3 loomed near, and he said it had been a tough quarter for the sales team. Last year, most of the team members nailed their quotas, and the organization overall came in above goal. In fact, sales were strong enough to carry revenue into the first quarter of the new year. But by midyear, the team's hot streak had cooled. The team was scrambling while its forecasts fell short of its goals. Everything had been great: "We're hot. Who needs a plan?" he said, describing the sentiment of the team until that time. Now they needed to do something—quickly.

Nobody liked to plan. Nobody liked to come in from the field and work through the challenges of devising strategies for reaching sales goals. When it came to planning for the accounts that made up about 70 to 80 percent of the company's revenue, the account managers and sales team members typically avoided it. The voices could be heard throughout the sales organization: "It's a pain." "It takes too much time out of market." "I'm a relationship person, not an operator." "Can't the sales support team put this together for us to react to?" When customer demand was strong and close rates were high, it was easy to find reasons why the team didn't need account plans. But when the dry spell hit, the head of sales realized that they were all victims of their success.

Account planning is one of those hot topics that receive a disproportionate amount of attention and create more than their fair share of heartburn for sales teams. It's is right up there with sales compensation, quotas, and coaching as disciplines that tend to catch the spotlight in sales meetings. Companies know they need to do account planning well, but don't. Most times, when the topic of account planning arises in a conversation, I hear:

- We don't do it well, but we really need to get better.
- We already do it. The key sections of the account plan are . . .
- We've tried it in the past, and it doesn't work because the team isn't on board.
- It turns out to be an administrative exercise, and once it's done, we end up putting it away until next year.
- It's critical. But we don't have time for it.

Notice that none of these responses outright diminishes the value of account planning. Effective account planning is one of the most powerful drivers of sales performance, yet it's one of the most overlooked because of its paradoxical relationship to sales: Many salespeople intuitively think that spending more time selling will create more sales. But the salespeople who invest in account planning as they sell actually sell more.

SalesGlobe research shows that the most successful sales teams combine consistent account planning with selling. Poor-performing or inconsistent sales teams typically have a pattern of reacting to opportunities and only planning in response to lagging results.

While implementing a strong account planning process sounds like a no-brainer, most sales organizations face these 10 questions:

1. How should account planning fit within our sales strategy?
2. What accounts should have account plans?
3. Who should own account planning?
4. How do we align functions such as marketing, operations, finance, and human resources?
5. What are the most important components of the account plan?
6. How should a good process work?
7. Can we make the organization conduct account planning, and how do we get compliance?
8. How can we reinforce the value of account planning?
9. How should the customer be involved in the process?
10. How do we keep the account planning process alive throughout the year?

Difficulties in answering these questions sideline the account planning process, hinder the sales organization's potential, and result in missed growth opportunities.

Essential Account Planning concentrates on the big challenges sales organizations face today regarding strategically planning for growth at the account level. This book addresses these challenges with practical approaches and tools you can apply right away with your sales teams to see results this year. It also includes stories, interviews, and wisdom from executives in leading companies about how they use account planning to grow their businesses.

This book begins by addressing why you need account planning in the first place. It will help you sort through the arguments you're certain to hear about organizational commitment, ownership, politics, and time. It will also help you make the case for account planning and how it fits into your broader sales strategy.

Then this book will look at the five keys for successful strategic account planning:

- **Key 1: Use the right structure (chapter 2).** This chapter will look at the big picture of the sales strategy, account plan vision, and account plan execution, as well as the components every good account plan should have.
- **Key 2: Set the goal (chapter 3).** This chapter will examine how the account plan supports the business plan and growth opportunities, and how to build the revenue goal for the account.
- **Key 3: Create the habits (chapter 4).** Without this key, the account plan is just a document. This chapter discusses how to bring the account planning process to life.
- **Key 4: Understand the politics (chapter 5).** At the core of the account planning process are the people who make it happen. This chapter examines the importance of getting the sales team and others within the company to work together to solve the people, role, and political challenges.
- **Key 5: Think big (chapter 6).** This chapter will focus on moving past incremental thinking and toward planning in an aspirational manner to take your team beyond its current horizons.

Essential Account Planning looks at each of the keys from the perspective of sales leaders and sales enablers by studying their stories, as well as the stories of hundreds of companies I've worked with in the past 25 years, to lay out methods to help your organization profit from these experiences. Once you've read about the five keys, you can use the templates included in the appendix in your account planning process.

I hope you enjoy the book and leverage it to improve your sales team's performance. Let me know about the challenges you're addressing or the results you're seeing by sending me a note at mark.donnolo@salesglobe.com or on Twitter @MarkDonnolo #EssentialAccountPlanning. I'd love to learn about your experiences.

Chapter 1

Why Do You Need Account Plans?

Last year, I found myself trapped in a conference room with a handful of people who clearly did not want to be there. I had flown to Dallas to help a midsized technology hardware company implement an account planning process. The company was starting the program from scratch—it had never had a formal account planning process before. And it was clear from the meeting the sales team did not think this process was necessary.

The sales executives were smart and seasoned. They were comfortable handling large strategic accounts—in their own way. And while revenue numbers were fine, the head of sales and marketing knew that with some planning, they could be great.

David seemed especially displeased to be there. He was the account leader for the plan we were working on, and he was the only one at the meeting wearing jeans and a golf shirt. He sat hunched over the conference table, resting his weight on his elbows, tapping a pen on his notebook.

Given that this was a $40 million account, the chief marketing officer and president of the business unit had both flown in for the meeting. Jennifer, the chief marketing officer, sat at the head of the table, looking down at the draft David had provided. "What was our revenue by product last year for this account?" she asked.

David snagged a doughnut from the tray on the table and leaned back in his chair. "I can get that for you this week," he said.

"OK," she said, and tried again. "Can you tell me the expected revenue by product for this year?"

"Well, we're not a tier one vendor," said David. "They just put those tiers in this year, so that limits us a little. But we have great relationships. I've known these guys for years. There's some realignment going on there, too, so I'm waiting to see how that will shake out. But these guys are my buddies."

One of the sales representatives, Scott, sat to David's right. As small in stature as David was large, Scott bounced in his black executive's chair. "We're going to get 50 percent of revenue from staff outsourcing," he said, grinning nervously. Jennifer glanced at me, looking concerned.

"But that's counter to our strategy," she said. "We want to move away from staff outsourcing and toward our new software product. The margins are shrinking with staffing. Is this 50 percent coming from current buying centers?"

David continued to recline in his chair. "Well right now, with the realignment of the client in October, we're trying to identify where the buying centers are and what the offers are."

Jennifer's eyes widened. It was February, and David didn't have a clue what was going on in his account. Worse, he didn't care. He hadn't taken the account planning meeting seriously at all; he had barely done the minimum preparation work, and he had not considered any ways to grow the revenue in the future. For the past five years, David had managed the account by building relationships and taking orders. But the company's wallet share was shrinking as competitors found new ways to go deeper into this client, and now the business was at risk. David was oblivious.

"These guys have some reorganization to work out," he repeated, as if Jennifer hadn't understood an important point. "Everything is on hold now." He sat up and leaned in toward me. "Can you remind me who plans to use this data, and how it will be used? My team and I have always managed this in the past, and I'm unclear why we need this documentation. We've got it up here," he said, tapping his temple.

"It's important to document the current state of the account and the goals of the account for your sales team and the rest of the organization," I began. From the corner of my eye, I could see Jennifer draw a deep breath. It was going to be a long morning.

As David was demonstrating for us, altering the methods of salespeople to include account planning was a daunting task. At the very least, we were asking them to transfer the notes and strategies from their head to paper; at worst, we were suggesting they lacked a strategic plan for the accounts they had worked on for years. The truth was, this account—and the other 20 strategic accounts we were planning—was critical for the business. And while David was keeping it afloat, it needed input from other sales and sales enablement teams to grow.

David's attitude toward account planning isn't unusual, and for the record, account planning indifference is hardly limited to salespeople. I see it at all levels, from the chief sales officer to field reps. But it's usually an opinion built by previous, failed account planning attempts.

Account planning is an essential part of a high-performing sales organization. It brings together critical information about your customer, competitors, and strategy to win business. The account plan forces the team to acknowledge the larger revenue and product goals and agree on a set of actions to move your team, inch by inch or mile by mile, toward those goals. And the plan serves as an accountability checkpoint. Have team members done what they said they were going to do? Have their activities brought you closer to your goals? If not, how does the team regroup, refresh, and continue forward?

Most sales organizations acknowledge this. Account planning sounds like a great idea (because it is). The problems start when you ask account leaders to stop what they're doing and focus on a plan. More problems arise when you expect multiple people to be involved in writing the plan—to stop calling on customers, sit down, and look up some numbers or competitive information. And then disaster strikes when you ask this same team to repeat the process, quarter after quarter, year after year. The act of incorporating a new activity—planning—into an already saturated schedule is tough. The route to making this planning into a long-term habit is crowded with obstacles.

But it's not impossible, and it's well worth the effort.

"Account planning is foundational, because if you don't know where you're going, any road will do," says Sue Holub, vice president of enterprise software marketing at Lexmark International. In my 25 years of working with hundreds of Fortune 1000 sales organizations, I've seen thousands of road options. Without a plan, companies trust their gut, which may or may not be based in fact; take the path of least resistance; or follow the same familiar road they've always taken.

Every sales organization is unique, but most have similar challenges and succeed using a common set of principles. All sales organizations can leverage the five keys laid out in this book as landmarks on their path to long-term account planning success and more predictable revenue growth. *Essential Account Planning* tackles each key and how it relates to implementing an effective account plan and establishing a living account planning process in your organization:

1. Use the right structure.
2. Set the goal.
3. Create the habits.

4. Understand the politics.
5. Think big.

Why Account Planning Is Urgent

Mike Barnes, executive vice president with Andrews Distributing, one of the largest beer distributors in the United States, knows the value of account planning. Several years ago, the company started to follow a structured account planning process. It collected large amounts of data about its customers' buying habits segmented by geography, and, based on what it learned, changed its sales coverage model. "The minute that we did that, we had the first year of consecutive months of share growth," says Barnes. "We're now in our third year, and as we have improved in account planning, we've seen our market share grow. We're in our 34th consecutive month of share growth—and that's virtually unheard of in our industry."

Account planning provides a structure to determine what's important and what's not when pursuing customers. As competition in markets increases, account plans become critical to reaching goals and achieving growth.

Here are five reasons why account planning can make a difference in your sales organization now.

Competition Is Out There

Markets across industries have become more competitive over the past 20 years. Most industries have experienced an increased number of competitors, some enabled by new technologies. There's also a higher level of sales talent due to the professionalization of sales careers and growing number of colleges and universities that offer degrees in sales. Customers are more intelligent and better informed about what they need. To beat the competition, you must know more about your customers, better understand their needs, have a differentiated value proposition, and have an actionable plan. Account plans provide data that pinpoint the market share, level of competition, and strengths and weaknesses of not only your position but also your competitors'—all of which contribute to predicting whether you can hit your goals.

Account plans demand that you acknowledge these challenges and define them specifically. Who are your competitors? How much market share do they have? What value do they offer? Account plans also require specific actions to overcome these challenges.

"The account planning process helps you develop a discipline to look for either early warning signs or potential opportunities, where you might not have seen them before," says Holub. "You start to become more resourceful, more insightful, more observational as a sales executive. That's an immediate benefit to account planning."

Account Plans Coordinate Teams

Most individual sales representatives are great at the tactical level. But accounts typically require larger coordination either between accounts or within the same account, depending on its size. Account plans also reveal how well you work with teams from different parts of the company to accomplish account goals. How does the sales team work with the technical organization? How do they work with the marketing organization or operations? Account plans help improve your capabilities because you're engaging many different parts of the company. Without account plans, sales operates by gut, and marketing, technical, and operations react without the advantage of a plan.

At InterContinental Hotels Group (IHG), multiple organizations touch every account. Sales enablement determines which accounts should be in a team's portfolio and collects intelligence for those accounts. Sales operations makes sure those accounts show up correctly in a rep's portfolio, and it supervises data entering and verification. Operations also works with the finance and sales teams to set the financial target for each account. The analytics team provides guidance for everyone. "It is a formal process, and it is well defined. It works well at IHG," says Scott Taylor, director of global sales operations and worldwide sales for IHG.

IHG isn't unusual. Without a coordinated effort, teams can't keep up with the amount of information passing through many hands.

In fact, David, from the beginning of this chapter, learned this lesson the hard way. Several months after my visit, David lost his job. His performance had fallen over the past year, and his lack of ability to embrace an account plan that could help him course-correct advanced his demise. His replacement, John, was a team player. He reached across many aisles in the company and gathered input from sales operations, sales leadership, marketing, and procurement. He rallied his team, including the wide range of adjuncts; built a strategic account plan; followed it; and grew the business.

The Account Is One Piece of a Larger Puzzle

Every company has financial goals, and stakeholders need to understand how the company is performing against those goals. Chief financial officers and other financial leaders must present this information and demonstrate that they have a plan to achieve those goals. But the sales organization—and usually only the sales organization—knows what's going on at eye level. Account plans help to communicate that bottom-up view. The sales organization has an opportunity to discuss what customers are doing, for better or for worse, and offer valuable information about how sales will achieve its goals.

Account Plans Create Accountability

The sales team needs a way to measure its success beyond whether individuals achieve their quota. The team needs metrics, goals, and milestones to work toward. Account plans create a record of what individuals are supposed to do—both the actions and the goals—which can be used in performance metrics: "You said you were going to close this $50,000 opportunity with ACME. Did you?" If not, you can look back at the activities that were supposed to lead to that sale: "You said you were going to call Don two months ago; you also said you'd ask for introductions to Betty and Bob in the production division. Did you?" If a rep has worked the plan and it still hasn't worked, it's her defense—she did what she was supposed to do, but the plan hasn't worked so far. This might mean it's time to tweak the plan. If she didn't, it's an opportunity for specific coaching on follow-through.

Account Plans Assess Sales Skills

Account plans act as a foundation for capability development. Do the salespeople have the skills to get to the correct buyer? If not, what type of training is needed? On which points in the account plan are account reps succeeding? On which points are they stumbling? Account plans can offer evidence of the types of training or coaching necessary at an individual and team level.

Andrews Distributing uses account plans to determine which reps have mastered their sales process and which need more training. One of the most difficult challenges in his sales organization, Barnes says, is determining rep capability. The Andrews account plans rely heavily on data, which increases the company's ability to move faster—from sales to operations to procurement.

"Asking the sales team to adapt at the pace we're changing is probably one of the toughest challenges we face," says Barnes. "There's diversity in ability." Consequently, Andrews has created a mentoring program for reps who need more coaching, and account plans identify reps who need help or can serve as mentors.

Account Plan Challenges

So how do companies end up in situations like the one at the beginning of this chapter, struggling through a painful account planning session that's obviously not valued by those involved? I've seen the following major challenges to achieving a well-oiled account planning process:

Lack of Commitment

When a process takes hold at a grassroots level and spreads throughout the organization, it creates a powerful result. For example, if sales teams adopt a new customer relationship management tool or a new account planning process, it can help those teams and eventually benefit the entire company. Unfortunately, for most companies that see a grassroots account planning movement, it doesn't gain commitment from everyone and, at some point, leaves a pattern of ad hoc practices that benefit a few teams but has little overall effect on results.

Account planning works best when the entire company stands behind the process, winning over even successful salespeople who can make their quotas by doing their own thing, who think that approach is a lot easier than stepping back and working on an account plan.

Andrews Distributing has been committed to its account planning process for 10 years, and it's affected every facet of the company. For the last two years, Mike Barnes and Mike McGuire, president of Andrews Distributing, have talked a lot about their portfolio of accounts. Their desire has always been to make sure they have prescriptive solutions so that their people have a better opportunity to be successful. For example, a rep might tell a customer, "If you replace this brand of beer with this brand, we anticipate a 20 percent increase in sales, based on these past trends." But Andrews doesn't work in a vacuum. They have numerous suppliers, brands of beer from Miller to Coors to Corona, and numerous SKUs. In any given sales meeting, reps are bombarded with information.

"How can they focus?" asks Barnes. "It's an energy drainer for the sales team, unless you have great account planning. And in the spirit of servant leadership, that's something we desire to do." As Barnes and McGuire talked about their mission to become a trusted adviser for their customers through indisputable data and insight, they had to plan for this information. Knowing more about their customers informed their decisions about hiring; their sales reps must have the right skill set to use the information.

Andrews committed to account planning at the C-level, but knew it was also crucial at the account leader level. "We tell our brand team, marketing service teams, and commercial marketing team: 'We should never, ever go forward with any strategy or plan unless the sales leaders own it first.' And then, it becomes a collaborative plan. If the sales leaders don't own it first, we're vulnerable right out of the chute. Nobody likes to have anything pushed to them that they don't own. Then we win together, we fail together, we learn together. There is power in being together on every mission, and every plan, and every strategy."

Whether the account planning process starts at the top or the bottom, the organization must have strong commitment from leadership. That commitment has to follow through to sales leadership, sales management, and each salesperson who has a role in the account planning process.

Weak Ownership

When working with sales organizations on sales process and roles, I ask, "Who owns the account strategy and the account plan?" The answer to this question tells me volumes about the team's effectiveness. I expect to hear a decisive and consistent answer across the organization and the accounts it covers. The plan owner might be the lead account manager, lead account executive, sales manager, or someone else in a leadership role with that account. But sometimes, I get inconsistent answers within a single sales organization. No one really knows who owns the account. Unclear ownership indicates a lack of accountability and a gap in leadership that can result in sales opportunities falling through the cracks. Designate ownership of the overall account planning process and the plans for each account.

Obtrusive Politics

Big quotas put pressure on revenue expectations. Control over revenue, especially big revenue in a strategic account, is valuable and can result in political behavior as people try to stake their claims and secure their resulting sales incentives. Politics often occur in an environment of perceived scarcity that creates competition for limited opportunities. If the team has effective account planning roles and processes, it gains the ability to think and work in an environment of abundance, dissolving the need for politics. Strong sales leadership can give the organization a more optimistic view of market opportunities and how account planning can help it take advantage of those opportunities.

The Account Planning Document

I asked a sales executive recently about how her team handles account planning, and she talked about how ineffective it was because people didn't complete all the requisite sections. When I first discuss account planning with a sales team, members typically talk about the document they produce, the sections, how often they create it, and how laborious and painful the process is.

However, account planning shouldn't be about the document. It's about the client needs, the innovative ideas to meet those needs, a committed plan to address those needs, and the discipline of ownership and execution from the team. Elevate the position of account planning beyond the document. The document merely contains all the hard work, and it will continue to evolve as the work and results progress.

Selling, Not Planning

Most salespeople love the pursuit. They don't love planning. They'd rather sit in front of a customer than plan how to sit in front of a customer. And yet the most successful sales teams I've worked with understand the criticality of account planning, and they embrace it. They link effective account planning with results in their accounts—usually big results. If a salesperson isn't a planner and thinks incrementally and transactionally, she is likely to get incremental and transactional results. If she thinks big and is intentional about operating according to the plan, she will make different, longer-term decisions and see greater results.

As part of its account plans, Andrews Distributing asks reps to count the display cases in every grocery store. So reps walk up and down the aisles, noting locations where Andrews might possibly showcase beer, to understand how they're executing at every display location within every grocery store they have. They enter the data into their account plans. The idea is each rep is always looking for opportunities in each store, even if it's not obvious at first.

Interestingly, Barnes discovered that not all methods of counting beer were the same. "We had 200 salespeople with potentially 30 different ways they count beer," says Barnes. "So, we had to establish one way to count beer—and that alone was a lot of change. Everybody said that their way of counting was the best way. Today, we're all counting one way. Our execution on counting by location has gone from 40 percent compliance to 95 percent compliance," says Barnes.

While counting display cases—and then learning how to count beer—may seem to take away from the reps' selling time, Barnes says it's made the reps more effective: "The goal of this activity is to make sure we optimize their selling time." The information collected goes into the account plan and creates a filtered, pre-prescribed list of beer for each location. Without this planning, "reps are trying to figure it out along the way, and that's distracting from the optimal time to sell and service the account," says Barnes.

Contrary to instinct, the work of account planning will take you farther than trying to pull it off yourself. Investing the time to do a good account plan increases the value exponentially.

Account Planning in Context of the Sales Organization

Most likely, you'll need new habits to make account planning successful in your organization. But you don't have to start from scratch. Chances are, sales reps already perform many of the tasks, albeit on the fly or independent of others in your sales organization. Account planning fits securely into structures and processes that probably already exist in your sales organization.

In 2014, ATD designed a World-Class Sales Competency Model (Figure 1-1), which describes the relationships among sales management and leadership, sales enablement, and the sales force. The model demonstrates points of intersection between these groups (sales leaders, sales trainers, sales operations, sales compensation experts, and sales coaches) and these activities. If you follow this model, your company has likely already laid the groundwork for successful account planning. You just need to put the pieces together, create the habits, and overcome power struggles or internal politics.

The following components of the World-Class Sales Competency Model outline parts of sales that you probably already have a strategy or plan for.

Sales Management and Leadership

Sales management and leadership, situated precisely in the middle of sales force and sales enablement, set the vision and establish the strategy for the sales force, and manage both the sales force and sales enablers to get the important work done.

Sales Strategy Definition and Execution

Account planning starts with the sales strategy. The strategy is the combination of what you sell (your products and services), to whom you sell (target customer or prospect base), and your value proposition. The strategy defines the sales organization's action plan to achieve its goal.

It also defines segmentation and targeting. What are the most lucrative opportunities on the market? What opportunities best fit your organization?

What will your value proposition be? What makes you unique? Why should a customer select you over a competitor? Account plans will then execute upon that strategy. Each major account is like a piece of the overall sales strategy puzzle. They all connect and work together to fulfill the sales strategy.

Figure 1-1. ATD World-Class Sales Competency Model

ATD's World-Class Sales Competency Model describes the relationships among sales management and leadership, sales enablement, and the sales force. Companies with similar structures are well in position for successful account planning.

Sales Team Management

Sales team managers lead and manage the sales organization in pursuit of the strategy. All the competencies that need to happen within the sales force and sales enablement areas don't happen automatically. They are the result of strong leadership and strong execution. Sales management should consider all the competencies in this model to make sure they are operating according to a well-defined system, leveraging an effective account planning process to get to their goal.

Sales Force

On the sales force side of the model, sales leaders and individual sales representatives are already focusing on the following activities, which are the basic components of effective account planning.

Sales Pipeline Forecast and Management

Account plans help build your pipeline with specific opportunities. They help with forecasting because the plans increase visibility on what you can sell. Given that, you can move into how the accounts in the plan support that strategy. Each account will make up a piece of that strategy.

New Account Acquisition and Account Development and Retention

Acquisition, development, and retention represent the universe of ways to grow the business organically. You can acquire another company to grow, but otherwise your accounts should comprise your overall account strategy. These types of accounts will be the bulk of account planning because they are the most significant accounts in organizations.

When you look at the buildup of all the accounts that make up the fulfillment of the sales strategy, some of it will come from the acquisition of customers that you're not working with right now. Some part of the strategy—usually the bulk—will be made up of the retention and development of existing accounts. Both new accounts and the development of existing accounts represent additional buying points and additional usage of your products and services.

Complex Solution Definition and Positioning

The next areas—complex solution definition and positioning—define what solutions you're going to offer those accounts, based on what they need. Not all solutions are complex. In major account situations, however, the customer often is well informed and knows the solution needed. It's the job of the rep to listen and respond to the customer's needs. Your solution should be based not on what you think the market needs, but what the customer actually needs and what you can fulfill. In an account plan, don't dictate the solution. It's a common mistake; you have a portfolio of solutions you want to sell to the account. The better method is to put yourself in the customer's shoes during account planning and ask, "What is the customer dealing with? What solutions will solve these problems?" Solutions will run the range from standard and transactional to complex and highly customized. All should be considered during the account planning phase and verified or revised throughout the course of customer interaction.

Partner Sales Support

Partners can be an integral part of the account plan, especially in complex accounts for which you can't offer the full solution or don't have access to the right buyers. Partners can accelerate your growth in an account by collaborating to meet a mutually beneficial goal. Usually, your best partners are going to be complementary to your business in terms of what they offer or where they play in the sales process. For example, a technical services organization may leverage relationships with a consulting firm to gain access and provide software implementation services. The partnership helps the technical services company round out its offers and grow revenue, and it helps the consulting firm by bringing in new customers.

Sales Enablement

On the sales enablement side of the model, the sales leaders, sales trainers, and sales operations people are already planning for sales' success through the following:

Sales Coaching

Sales coaches work week to week with account team members to keep them on track. Coaches also use the account plan as a road map of activities to assess sales skills and develop any lagging capabilities to work with the account. And they continually coach the skills necessary for strategic planning, rather than allowing reps to fall back into transactional mode.

Sales Talent Selection

It's important to select the right people for each role in the sales organization. You need different characteristics: people with strengths that range from sales execution to sales enablement and support to account leadership and account team support. Identify the characteristics for the optimal person in each role, and identify new talent to fill any gaps when necessary. Account plans put all these roles into action. As with David, from the beginning of the chapter, the practice of account planning can expose an account leader or team member who's not the right fit. Creating accountability through the account plan can prevent ineffective members from hiding amid the complexity of the account and ultimately improve results for the company.

Sales Talent Development

It is important to build the skills of the account team through coaching, as previously mentioned, or through formal sales training. When you're selecting talent, you look for people best matched to the optimal role, or you build skills to get your existing team to the optimal role and beyond. The reality is that not everyone will meet the optimal role standard from the beginning, so you have to implement some sales training. Talent development also builds consistency among processes within the organization. If you need to develop new solutions, you don't want salespeople to determine that individually; you want to leverage best practice methodologies.

Sales Tool and Process Improvement

Sales tools further enable account plans to capture information and assist with planning, measuring, and managing performance within the account. Pipeline management and forecasting tools are common, but you can also use buyer mapping and solution development tools. The organization will often define the requirements for its sales tools based on its strategy and account plans, and then either source those tools from third parties or develop them in-house.

Sales Incentive and Compensation Design

Incentive and compensation connect the sales strategy to frontline sales performance. The organization may want to be more specific about how it motivates the attainment of account-specific goals. These could include sales of strategic products or attainment of significant milestones in accounts with very long sales processes. However, any sales compensation program that incorporates account plan objectives should be part of an overall architecture of sales compensation, not developed ad hoc in the field. Don't go rogue and start tweaking incentive plans.

Account plans help coordinate the sales force and sales enablement sides of the model. Without an account plan, some of the activities will be done by some of the people, some of the time. But all of the activities will not be done by all of the people all of the time unless there's a plan in place and it's regularly followed.

People make the process work. You can have an account plan structure and an account planning process, but if you don't engage people properly it's all academic. One of the problems with account planning is that just about everyone in your sales organization knows how to do an account plan. The magic of account planning happens when you engage people correctly and it becomes a living account planning process. Account plans live and die based on how committed people are to the process and how well that process ultimately shows business results with the account.

Which Accounts Require Plans?

In general, companies create account plans for customers that are larger and more complex, and warrant the investment to grow. The strategic accounts together—as a segment—typically make up a majority of a company's revenue.

Companies often use the Pareto Principle to determine which accounts satisfy these requirements. The Pareto Principle, named after economist Vilfredo Pareto, is often called the 80/20 rule. It says that 80 percent of the output comes from just 20 percent of the input. In terms of sales, this means that often 80 percent of a company's revenue comes from 20 percent of its customers. When deciding which accounts to select for account planning, you'd want to know the 20 percent of accounts that generate roughly 80 percent of your revenue. Figure 1-2 illustrates a Pareto analysis in which roughly 20 percent of accounts comprise roughly 80 percent of the company's revenue and gross margin.

To do this for your own company, sort accounts in descending order from largest to smallest and look at the current revenue. You'll eventually get to a point where you've grouped together enough accounts to make up between 60 and 80 percent of your company's revenue. This percentage will vary based on the inflection point of the Pareto curve. So, if there's a large amount of revenue captured by a small number of accounts and then it drops off dramatically, that's usually where the company will draw the line.

Figure 1-2. Pareto Analysis

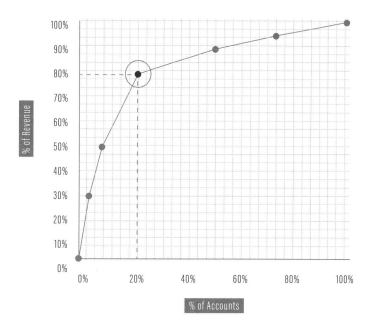

The Pareto Principle shows that roughly 80 percent of a company's revenue comes from roughly 20 percent of its customers. In the Pareto Analysis here, the curved line tracks the revenue from each account; the dotted line illustrates the inflection point at which customer revenue per account begins to decline significantly. In this case, exactly 80 percent of the company's revenue comes from exactly 20 percent of its customers.

I worked with a communications technology company a couple of years ago that was struggling to get growth results from its global accounts. My team and I evaluated the sales organization, listened to the customer, and ran the analytics. We found many opportunities for improvement, but there was one major problem that needed immediate attention: The organization had 200 global accounts in its portfolio. However, a global account team cannot possibly focus on 200 accounts. We looked at the Pareto analysis and found that a full 90 percent of the company's revenue came from 20 accounts. The sales team tried to cover all 200; not surprisingly, this approach was ineffective. So as the team nervously watched, sales leaders and I cut global accounts down to 20, and moved the rest to what they called "strategic" accounts. Over the next year performance improved dramatically.

You can look at the Pareto with different metrics. For example, you could classify your accounts by current revenue, but you might overclassify smaller accounts with which you do a lot of business and underclassify accounts that have a lot of potential. Another view is to classify your accounts by potential revenue, which would include accounts that have a strategic fit within your business according to what you sell and your positioning.

Ecova, a utility and energy management company, selects its top 30 accounts by margin rather than revenue, for account plans that go into greater detail. As the company has matured, Seth Nesbitt, chief commercial officer, has seen a fairly large variation in margin per client. "It's something to think about when you're allocating resources during account planning," he says. "Consider what's really important in your business. For us, energy is very much a margin and EBITDA-driven [earnings before interest, tax, depreciation, and amortization] business."

It's easy for the sales team to want to focus on the highest-revenue-generating clients, but that metric does not always have the most impact on the business. "That was a big revelation for us, to go back and evaluate clients on EBITDA," says Nesbitt. "We partnered with finance during the account planning process, and in terms of prioritization, that exercise was critical for us. We could have missed some very important, high-margin clients just because they are not the high-revenue clients."

When deciding on which accounts to focus the brunt of your attention, determine the most important business performance metric. Those are the clients you want to grow and plan for profitable relationships.

5 Questions About How Account Planning Fits Into Your Sales Organization

1. Do you have leadership and team commitments to the discipline of account planning?
2. Does sales leadership effectively communicate the value of account planning, including messaging that investing the time to create a good account plan increases the value exponentially?
3. Does your sales organization focus on the account planning document, or have you elevated account planning to its execution and consistency?
4. Is your sales organization already using the World-Class Sales Competency Model?
5. When selecting accounts for account planning, are you choosing more than your team can effectively focus on?

Chapter 2

Use the Right Structure

We raced down the thin ribbon of highway through the open plains at about 130 kilometers per hour. Even at this speed, cars closed in on us from behind and flashed their brights before passing us on the two-lane road. After driving for a couple of hours, Gallo, my client, pressed on the brakes, slowing the Citroën as we approached the small town of Toro.

Gallo drove the car up the gravel road and navigated through the main gate. The road turned to cobblestone and we progressed slowly through the streets, winding between pedestrians and small cars. After a few turns, we pulled to the curb in front of a centuries-old building, which now housed a bank. Gallo gestured in front of the branch, pointing to the sign and the ATM, and then took me into the lobby, continuing to identify aspects of the interior design and signage. It was helpful when he gestured clearly because I hardly understood his rapid Spanish and he didn't speak English.

We were working on a major corporate identity and branding project for a large bank that had acquired six other banks, or *cajas,* to form a consolidated company in the Castilla-León region of Spain. Gallo and I had traveled to many cities, including Madrid, León, Valladolid, and now Toro, to look at the unique branding situations the company had, from ancient towns to suburbs to large cities. We had designed a corporate identity program for the bank that included its new trademark and applications such as credit cards, marketing collateral, advertising, and signage.

For the signage program, we needed to determine how the same sign would look in an international city like Madrid and a medieval town like Toro. Then, we had to determine the logistics of designing, manufacturing, and installing all the signs, ATM casings, and bank interiors so the bank could launch the new brand with a "big bang" and the public would experience a rapid brand change over a period of weeks.

To accomplish this, we worked within a framework of brand standards. While they sound potentially limiting, the brand standards and roll-out process prevent chaos. Designers call it "freedom within a framework." The framework ensures that the company has an effective and efficient approach. The freedom comes when the framework's users spend their energy being creative and coming up with new ideas. Within this framework, Gallo and I achieved our goals for the banks in Castilla-León: brand impact, clear communication of the positioning, consistency of application, and resource efficiency.

Account planning works the same way. A strong account planning program specifies the vision, account plan structures, and process the sales team will use. Gone are the days of one-off creations that are unclear, incomplete, ineffective, and time-wasting, and that result in missed opportunities. Here are the days of impact, communication, consistency, efficiency, and effectiveness, allowing the account team to spend its time and energy thinking about how to solve the client's problems creatively.

Big Picture Structure

Account plans don't exist as stand-alone tools; they fit within a larger sales effectiveness hierarchy (Figure 2-1). This chapter will look at the structure of the account plan, from the sales strategy and account plan vision set by the chief sales officer (CSO), to the execution of the plan by the field reps, to the provision of crucial information and the monitoring of results.

Sales Strategy

When executives talk about strategy, it can sound esoteric or academic. But the sales strategy is simply an action plan to achieve the sales goal. The strategy is usually set by the CSO with the support of sales leadership and sales operations, incorporating their insight about market needs. And while the CEO and CSO are rarely involved in the day-to-day activities of account planning, their insight is crucial at this high level because the account plans will become the building blocks of how the organization will tactically execute the strategy.

Sales strategy dictates your target customer segments; it determines what you're offering in terms of products and services, the value proposition to the customer, and your approach to market in terms of channels and sales resources. The strategy tells the sales organization how it should operate within each account.

Is there an emphasis on a new product? A new industry? A new go-to-market approach? Each account plan drives a piece of the strategy.

Figure 2-1. The Account Planning Team

Account planning is not just the responsibility of the account leader; the entire sales organization, sales enablement, and other functions all have significant roles to make account planning successful. The illustration above shows some of the critical teams and their roles.

A shift in sales strategy increased the importance of account plans at Merial, a global pharmaceutical company, says Brad Kaegi, senior director of marketing for the Pets EMEA region. For years, the veterinary industry was largely independent veterinary practices—90 percent of which Merial had penetrated with at least one product—and Merial designed a sales force to call on these practices. The sales organization mostly offered promotional resources to vets to help drive the business in Merial's different categories. Account planning focused on the share of wallet, and how sales could expand each practice. Sales leaders used a model that segmented practices based on potential for expansion within each account. They also had a tool integrated with their customer relationship management (CRM) system that helped create each plan, down to the number of calls reps would make and what kind of resources they were going to spend on each account.

A few large, conglomerate practices existed, but they were only about 10 percent of the market. The national sales organization managed these groups as a side job. In fact, before the large buying groups started growing in number, the sales organization could largely ignore them, and essentially had a "do nothing" strategy. They maintained a relationship, but never agreed to their pricing concessions because Merial was growing fast enough outside the regular market, and they just didn't need to.

Until they did. "Ten years ago, when I was on the national accounts team, there was a large hospital organization," says Kaegi. "They came to us and said, 'We're very excited; we want to talk to you about your flea and tick products.'"

"We thought, 'We're the market leader. We have our strategy: Create great products, gain veterinary recommendation, drive consumer demand into the veterinary practice, and spin that cycle of demand.' We looked at the sales opportunity and thought, 'This is great.'" So Kaegi and the sales team put a proposal together for how they would support them with marketing efforts and included some minor price concessions.

"In retrospect, I don't even know if they considered us," he says. "They just used our offer to go beat up their preferred supplier. . . . We were just put in there to get some comparable negotiating power." Kaegi says it was a significant event for the company. Rather than ignoring the large organizations, Merial realized they needed strategic plans—plans that acknowledged the differences from the small independent practices. So the sales organization created a way to work with larger entities. And, of course, "the strategy changes meant that strategic planning became more important," says Kaegi. Over the last 15 years, a sales rep's book of accounts has decreased from 400 accounts to about 90 to allow for a greater focus on each.

Account Plan Vision

The company's vision for the account plan is not the same as its strategy (although both are usually set by the CSO). Vision converts the strategy to a method for getting it done. For example, a CSO might say, "Our sales strategy is to focus within our current accounts. We've had a 30 percent retention of customers historically, and we want to increase that to 50 percent. We want to concentrate on our customers that have $500 million to $5 billion in annual revenue. We want to increase renewals of our current software, sell our new software portfolio, and bundle it with our hardware products." That's sales strategy. It defines to whom you're selling, how you're selling to them, and what you're selling to achieve the sales goal.

The account plan vision outlines what the process will look like. This time, the CSO will consider which accounts to select for account planning; what information to include in the plans; how much detail each plan should include; how sales will work with other functions, including marketing and operations; and how the review process will work. For example, the CSO might say, "We will have an account plan for our top 20 accounts. I want the plans to be simple: 10 pages maximum. I want the account leader to own the plan, and teams will present to sales leadership quarterly."

The CSO's leadership philosophy and style influence the vision, as does the organization's culture. Some CSOs are very process oriented, while others are looser and more shoot-from-the-hip. Whatever the style, the CSO has to own the vision for account planning to work. It's her responsibility to define what role account planning will play in the organization. If the CSO doesn't commit to it, the sales operations team or sales leaders might, but most likely the plans will be inconsistent.

Above all, the vision should communicate that account planning will follow a single process, employ a single template, and be mandatory. The CSO has to communicate an unswerving message that account planning is essential to growth, quarter after quarter, year after year. If not, your competitors will all too happily fill the gaps carelessly left by the sales organization. If you don't have a plan for your top accounts, you can be sure your competitors will.

Account Plan Execution

Once the strategy and vision have been set, sales leadership and sales enablement can take that vision and turn it into a process. The owner of the account planning process can vary across companies, from the director of sales to a sales operations leader to an especially diligent sales rep. However, there is only one right answer: the account leader. The account leader is the person who owns the ultimate quota for that account and who works directly with those customers. He is responsible for the results and how the team works together to get those results.

Typically, sales leadership and sales enablement work together to create an account plan template and define what information needs to be included. Then, the account leader works with each of the supporting functions, including marketing, product development, and sales operations, to collect that information. The account leader is responsible for putting the plan together with each of them over a period of 30 to 60 days. The idea is to do as much of the work up front as possible and include as much relevant information as possible, before the account planning meeting. That way, once the key people are in the room for the actual meeting—many of whom have traveled great distances—the account plan is not a surprise. In an ideal world, the account leader has collaborated so much that the final plan is a confirmation that the team is on the right page and is in concert with the overall strategy, rather than a presentation of new information.

The 6 Components of Account Plans

Account plans vary in length, although their length doesn't necessarily speak to their quality. The best plan is one that creates a healthy tension between being clear and action-oriented and having enough detail to describe the strategy. The following six components encapsulate a best practice account plan for any organization. Determine the level of detail that works best for your culture and bandwidth, remembering that time spent gathering insight and planning specific actions saves time in the field. For each of these components, examples and templates are included in the appendix for you to use. Figure 2-2 illustrates the six components of an account plan.

Figure 2-2. The 6 Components of Account Plans

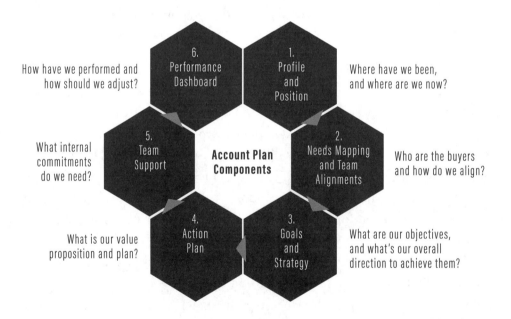

There are six major components to an account plan. Depending on the size and complexity of the account, information for all of these components can fit into a one-page account plan or may require a much longer plan. Tailor the information in these components to include critical insight for the account, while not creating an unreasonable workload for the sales teams. Above all, you want to make sure the account plan is used on a regular basis.

Profile and Position

Profile and position gives an overview of the account and the strengths and weaknesses of the relationships. It answers the questions, "Where have we been, and where are we now?" It includes four sections.

History

Your history with the account from a financial, buyer, and product or service perspective includes the:

- **Addressable market.** Look at the customer as a market. The addressable market is the customer's total annual spending for services that your company can provide. For some businesses, this information might be known at a high level, such as total IT or software spending if you're selling technology services. For other businesses, this information may be harder to come by. You could estimate the total addressable market by getting information directly from the customer or from competitors about what's purchased, and then use that to estimate total spending. You might even look at comparable companies and apply that to your customer. The addressable market is important to know because it represents the size of the pie. While you probably don't offer all the products and services to devour the whole pie, theoretically at least, that revenue is out there.

- **Current pipeline.** The pipeline reveals information about your current pursuits and progress within the account. This is useful to understand where you have momentum and where you can build. If your organization uses a CRM system accurately, good pipeline information should be easy to obtain.

- **Financial summary.** A financial summary shows the historic performance in the account from different perspectives, including prior years' revenue, bookings, profit, and performance to plan or budget. From this information, you may also look at multiyear trends and breakouts by product or offer. The objective is not to have a data dump of financial reports. It's to determine what you'd like to understand about your performance with the account and then identify the data and reports that will best tell the story.

Competitive Landscape

This landscape includes competitors by offer, value propositions, strengths, and vulnerabilities (appendix 1). The competitive landscape can be organized by offer, ranking your top competitors. You can also describe the competitive landscape in terms of the competitor's value proposition for each product, and strengths and vulnerabilities for each product. A competitive landscape, ranked by competitors' share of the account, can give you a clear view on what you're up against. It can also fuel some good conversations about what those competitors do to be successful in the account.

Customer Performance

This area includes a financial summary for the past year, such as Yahoo! Finance or Hoover's outputs or reports generated by your sales intelligence teams, and stock performance. (For privately held companies, this information might be difficult to obtain.) It's also valuable to create an overview of the customer's known challenges and priorities, because it can give you an initial view of opportunities to help (appendix 2). You can drill down into these opportunities later when you get into the goals and strategy section.

SWOT

Finally, include a classic analysis of your strengths, weaknesses, opportunities, and threats with this customer (appendix 3). Remember, the SWOT analysis is from your company's perspective. (I've seen companies mistakenly complete the SWOT from the customer's perspective, listing the customer's strengths, weaknesses, opportunities, and threats in the marketplace. Don't mix these up.) What are your company's specific strengths regarding this customer? For example, perhaps you are one of only several companies that can provide this particular product to your customer's technical specs. If you're close to your customer and have a trusted coach in the account, ask for a SWOT analysis of your company. It might shine a light on your blind spots.

Needs Mapping and Team Alignments

Needs mapping and team alignments describes your understanding of the customer needs and organizational alignments of your team to the account. It answers the question, "Who are the buyers and how do we align?" It includes three sections.

Summary of Customer Needs as an Organization

Describe the customer's top three to five needs. Then for each business unit or division, identify the customer's top three to five needs (appendix 4). This drills down into the customer challenges and priorities in the profile and position section.

Your Account Team

Lay out the team that works with the account, including people beyond sales (Figure 2-3). Successful account teams extend to sales, sales support, operations, customer service, and marketing.

You can also create an account map of buyers and your team (appendix 5). This tool exposes who you know in the account and who you don't. I've seen more than one account team go through this exercise and reveal strong relationships in only one division, or relationships at junior levels. It serves as a nice prompt to build relationships at missing levels.

On the customer side, the account map lists each person's role in the buying decision, your team's relationship strength, how frequently you contact them, what they buy, and the value of those purchases. It then asks what else they could buy and what their top challenge is.

On the team alignment side, the account map aligns your team to each person in the account. It specifies the role of each team member with that person, the value each team member should provide, and how each team member should coordinate with the rest of your team. For example, if one of the customer executives is the senior vice president of operations (SVP), you may align your division vice president (DVP) with that executive. Your DVP would know her role with the account, what value she should provide to the SVP, and how she should interact with your account team.

Figure 2-3. The Account Team

List the people from your company needed to help grow this account. Team members will likely include people from sales, sales enablement, and other functions.

White Space Map

The white space map gives your team a bird's-eye view on what you currently provide to the account for each buying point, business unit, or division (appendix 6). It lays out the set of offers on one axis and the buying points on the other. Each cell identifies what the customer purchases and current revenue levels (white spaces indicate no revenue or revenue below a certain threshold). You can grade the cells by high, medium, or low penetration. Of course, some buying points won't be candidates for all offers, but a good white space map will give a graphical representation of underdeveloped opportunities.

Goals and Strategy

This is where account plans start to get exciting. You've identified your current state, charted your past performance, mapped your alignments to the buyers in the account, and developed an initial understanding of the customer's needs. The goals and strategy component describes your overall objectives for the account, and how you will get to your goal. It answers the question, "What are our objectives, and what's our overall direction to achieve them?" It includes the goal build that takes the overall growth objective for the account and builds up the components of how the team's going to reach that objective (appendix 7). I detail the goal build exercise in chapter 3.

Action Plan

The action plan takes each component of the goal build and develops a tactical plan to achieve the goal. It answers the question, "What is our plan to achieve each opportunity?"

For each opportunity identified in the goal build, the action plan includes the challenge the customer is trying to address, a summary of your strategy, key steps, timing, and accountabilities (appendix 8). Start by confirming the customer's top challenge. Then describe your unique value proposition that responds to that challenge. From there, describe your overall account strategy. A good strategy answers what you are going to accomplish, who is going to accomplish it, and the resources you need. Finally, chart the action plan that describes each step in terms of the action, owner, and timing to accomplish the overall account plan objectives. There will be an action plan for each of the major opportunities your team identified in the goal build. Once completed, the team and executives can manage to the plan.

Team Support

Team support describes how your organization needs to come together across functions to support the account plan. It answers the question, "What internal commitments do we need?"

It includes the internal dependencies for the strategy across delivery, innovation, marketing, finance, legal, HR, and other organizations. By identifying dependencies and required support, you've established the conditions you need, such as a stable economic environment or passage of certain regulations, and your expectations of the investments from the company that will be required to accomplish the goals in the plan (appendix 9). For example, you may require new team members in sales and support roles to have the capacity to work with all the decision makers. You may also require certain investments, such as the funding of a new offshore operations center that can fulfill what you're selling to the client at a lower cost.

Performance Dashboard

The performance dashboard sets milestones and tracks your progress to those milestones; it also helps identify any adjustments that need to be made (appendix 10). It answers the questions, "How have we performed? How should we adjust?" It includes the following sections:

- dashboard with dimensions for each tactical action plan component (action, timing, and accountability)
- commitments, updated regularly for each tactical action plan component
- financial, offer, and buyer goals and year-to-date progress toward those goals
- actual performance to goal by division, product, and so on.

Note that the performance dashboard section may be hosted online for full access and visibility by the team and executives.

Living Account Planning Process

There are several primary functions of an account plan. The first is to make sure that all parties understand where the account is going. Second, it gives the salesperson the opportunity to show the rest of the sales organization that he has command of the client: He understands the strategy, and he has a plan for where the account relationship should go.

However, one of the most important reasons to hold an account planning meeting is to ensure that every other support group within the company understands its role in executing the plan and advancing the relationship. Everyone has to buy into it.

"We often say it takes a village to manage and grow large relationships," says David Long, vice president of strategic sales at LexisNexis, an information and risk management company. "It's not a single rep calling on a single buyer. Our relationships are very complex. You've got multiple buyers and multiple operation centers and multiple locations. And our product suite is pretty exhaustive. It takes the whole organization to advance us and move us forward. And if everyone comes out of that planning meeting understanding what their role is in advancing that particular relationship, then it's a success."

The execution of the account plan has to be an ongoing process (Figure 2-4). Quarter after quarter, year after year, account plans must be discussed and consulted. It's not enough to do it once and file the plan away in the dark corners of your hard drive. Chapter 4 discusses specific steps for creating account planning habits, but here are steps to get the account planning cycle off the ground.

Figure 2-4. Living Account Planning Process

Follow these seven steps to establish an account planning process in your organization.

Step 1. Assemble the Team

Senior sales leadership defines roles for the account planning team, identifies the types of people who need to be involved with account planning, and communicates those roles to the organization. These are strategic and structural decisions. Usually the CSO won't get to the level of designating individuals on the team. Instead, the account leader, backed by the authority of the senior sales leader, organizes the team. Team roles may need to be reinforced by sales leadership if the account leader is trying to engage people but encountering resistance, especially if the resisters are across functions outside of sales. The following people typically comprise your team:

Chief Sales Officer or Senior Sales Executive

The top sales executive who has established the account plan vision creates the mandate, sets the direction and tone, defines the overall process, and is the ultimate point of accountability. If the team isn't driving the process, this person also needs to be the hammer to come down in the appropriate places to drive things ahead.

Account Leader

The account leader drives the strategy and account planning process for the account. Depending on the level of seniority and authority of the account leader, she may select team members, work across functions to coordinate activities, and hold people accountable for development and execution of the account plan.

Regional or Local Sales Team Members

Salespeople responsible for driving the strategy under the leadership of the account leader may be account managers, sales representatives, product specialists, or industry specialists who provide focus and leadership on achieving key parts of the plan in the areas of customer business units, geographies, or particular product, service, and partner initiatives.

Sales Operations

Sales operations is the backbone of sales enablement, and supports the sales organization in attaining its goals. Depending on the organization, sales operations may be the managers of the process, coaches for planning, and support for making it a living process throughout the year.

Finance

The finance team plays a critical role in account planning by performing functions that may include providing information on account financial performance, conducting financial analytics, and supporting the account team with building its financial plan and forecasts.

Marketing and Product Marketing

With account planning, marketing provides the intelligence, strategic support, forecasting, and analytics around customers and offers. Marketing can help the account team understand customer performance, identify white space for untapped opportunities, and sharpen the value proposition. Marketing can also play an executional role by providing on-the-ground support in front of customers with programs such as customer-targeted collateral and newsletters, industry forums, and customer training.

Operations and Delivery

The operations and delivery teams implement solutions within strategic accounts, so they need to be participants in the account planning process rather than uninformed bystanders. As the team develops the plan, operations and delivery help determine how to meet demand and fulfill the value proposition. These teams also play a key role in developing and making new value propositions a reality in partnership with marketing and sales. As the account team gains a better understanding of customer needs, operations and delivery can help craft new or custom offers to meet those needs.

Once the team has been established and the roles confirmed by senior leadership, it's time to begin writing the account plan.

This is the opportunity for each of the players on the team to convey confidence in the organization, command a complex customer relationship, and work together to drive it forward. For better (account growth) or for worse (customer challenges), the cross-functional account team is in it together.

Role of the Customer

While the C-level sets the strategy and the vision, and sales leaders own and execute the plan, there's another vitally important player in this process: the customer. Your customers are at the center of the sales strategy—they're the reason you're running the business. While including the customer sounds like an obvious step, many sales organizations treat account planning as an internal operation and never involve their customers. However, if you don't consider the voice of the customer, your plan will be one-sided and could be dangerously off. For each of your target segments, the voice of the customer should tell you what they are looking for, how well you respond, and how you stack up against competitors. Involving the customer can help you identify gaps you may have in your performance. The customer also plays an important role in the development of the account plan—discussing your goals for the account and how you're going to work with it.

At Merial, sales reps work directly with the customer to develop the account plan. "The rep is not doing the planning by themselves, they're doing it with the customer so it's understood," says Kaegi. The account leader creates account plans with his customers for each of his top 20 accounts. "The big accounts where you're investing resources, that's where you do it together with the customer."

And customers appreciate the effort. Merial surveys its customers every two years, and customer feedback indicates Merial is "the most business-minded, trying to add value to each clinic," according to Kaegi. "The reps who get better revenue results get higher marks around their business planning piece. The customer attributes the formal account planning process to the fact that we're trying to add value to their business."

Step 2. Host a Kickoff Meeting

The purpose of the kickoff meeting is to introduce the team to the account planning process (or update the team on the process for a new year), the timing, and the accountabilities. The account leader shares the account plan template, discusses the components, and lays out the pre-work. The outcome of the kickoff meeting should be alignment to a clear set of objectives and an understanding of how the team will work together.

Step 3. Conduct Pre-Work

The first two components of the account plan, profile and position and needs mapping and team alignments, should be completed prior to the in-person account planning session. These sections give an overview of your past and present relationship with the account and provide critical insight for the rest of the account plan. The account leader usually assigns pre-work to team members according to their particular role.

For example, finance and marketing have pre-work related to the current state of the account. Consider establishing a capability so that finance and marketing can provide this information to different account teams easily. The account leader shouldn't have to spend too much time researching customized information, especially if your organization has finance and marketing experts who probably already have the information or can easily provide it. Sales operations, finance, and marketing should provide a standard package of current state analytics for each account, including the customer's addressable market, historic performance with your company, and the customer's current financial performance. Marketing should provide information about the customer's strategic priorities. That way, during the meeting the team can discuss ideas because you already have the insight.

Sales team members should assemble information for the SWOT analysis with input from marketing. The sales team should also put together information on account mapping: Who are the contacts? What is the strength of the relationship? What is our alignment to those contacts? For example, who within our organization has the relationship with each person in the customer's company? Do we need to pull in our CEO to strengthen the relationship with the customer company's CEO? You're not getting into strategy or the goal at this point, just the setup.

Finally, before the in-person meeting, the account leader has to confirm the completion of the pre-work. I've sat through more than one account planning session in which it was clear that no one had done the homework. The conversations are limited and are based on guesses: "I know competitor X is there, but I'm not sure what they're working on." It's critical that the insight is gathered before people clear their schedules and get on a plane for this meeting.

Step 4. Hold an Account Planning Meeting

The objective of the account planning meeting is to work with the team to get deep into the strategy. The team works through the goal build, actions and tactics, and the internal support. This meeting usually takes place in the fourth quarter of your fiscal year. The revenue goal for the account may or may not have been set yet, so it's possible you're working with a hypothetical goal during the meeting. Some organizations choose to work as teams virtually by videoconference or conference call. Some choose to work together in person. Technology is a powerful tool, but it doesn't replace the interaction and collaboration that comes with putting the team in a room. There's total focus, and each person makes a valuable investment in the team by spending the time together, which tends to increase engagement and improve performance. Once the team has developed a tight working relationship, technology like web conferencing is a great way to supplement and leverage those relationships. Of course, some organizations simply don't have the resources to fly account team members to the meeting. In those cases, leveraging technology is critical to working together.

Step 5. Finalize the Plan

After the in-person meeting, the team should have a batch of action items. It's ultimately the account leader's responsibility to manage those action items and hold team members accountable. While the account leader is responsible for a quality, actionable outcome, she may also get support from sales operations to make sure the team is on schedule. The account leader puts together the final account plan and prepares her team to present to leadership. She will also prepare the abridged executive version of the account plan, used for presentations.

Step 6. Present to Leadership

This meeting usually happens once a year as a major presentation to company leadership that may include the CSO, chief marketing officer, chief financial officer, president, and sometimes the CEO. While the team looks for an outcome of getting approval for the strategy and actions, a lot of the value is getting input and a strong critique from senior executives about how the plan supports the company strategy and whether the team is pushing the plan far enough. In some organizations, the account team may have interim presentations to leadership at midyear or quarterly points, depending on the significance and situation in the account.

Step 7. Execute the Plan

Once the account plan has been approved by senior leadership, the real process begins. It's time to execute the tactics you and your team agreed upon. Advise the team on the dates and the accountabilities for each of the phases in the account plan.

The Four Types of Account Plans

Let's take a quick look at the four types of account plans: strategic, tactical, aspirational, and pursuit (Figure 2-5).

Strategic Account Plan

This is the most common type of account plan. It's for large, complex accounts, typically the ones that represent the majority of your revenue (as determined by the Pareto Principle). They are designed to grow strategic accounts, whether global or national, and will have all six components.

Figure 2-5. Account Plan Types

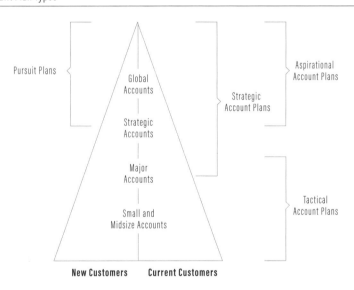

The four most common types of account plans are strategic, tactical, aspirational, and pursuit plans. Strategic, tactical, and aspirational account plans focus on retaining and growing revenue from current customers, while pursuit plans are used to win new business. Strategic account plans are typically used for global accounts, strategic accounts, and major accounts. Tactical account plans are used for smaller or less complex accounts, including some major accounts and small and midsize accounts. Aspirational account plans are less common, and only used for accounts that have very large revenue potential, which is usually limited to global and strategic accounts. Finally, pursuit plans typically focus on winning new business in global and strategic accounts.

Strategic accounts require involvement from many different groups: sales, marketing, sales operations, product development, customer care, and possibly

IT and legal. But sales has to lead the process and drive top-line revenue for that account. Strategic accounts can often be so large they put a lot of demand on your organization, beyond the sales teams. Account leaders have to be cognizant of that fact and plan for it during the account planning process. Will you offer a discount for this customer? What type of internal resources do you need to support the business? What other impact will the account have on the organization? How do you pull those people into the account planning sessions to get not only their assistance, but also their buy-in?

Tactical Account Plan

If an account is worth pursuing it's worth having some type of plan, but not all accounts warrant a comprehensive strategic account plan. In the case of midsized accounts, companies often use a tactical plan, which is a simplified version of the strategic account plan. A tactical plan is typically captured in one to three pages, which lay out the goals and tactics for the account.

Merial uses tactical plans for its smaller accounts where the sales process is highly transactional. For example, many of its top vaccine salespeople follow tactical account plans. Each sales rep creates a tactical plan for his top 20 accounts. The sales cycle is long, but it's fairly predictable for each account from year to year. Reps have a planning document, designed by sales leadership, that they work through with the veterinary practice owner or the decision maker in each practice.

It's an annual plan and they break it down into quarterly actions. "It is straightforward, and pretty simple," says Kaegi. "Some reps include a lot of detail, but it's pretty high level." Merial uses a two-page form that is primarily a checklist, including options for the veterinary practice to participate in many of Merial's promotional campaigns for its products. "It's mostly tick-boxes, planning and dates, and a calendar. There are some places for writing, but most of it is designed to be simple and less time-consuming for the rep," says Kaegi.

Before the standard tactical account plan, there was inconsistent account planning: "You had some reps that created plans in an Excel file, and they had a high level of detail; and then you had some of them that were just showing up, and they didn't really have a plan. So, we tried to bring together the planning process and make it simple, so it didn't seem too burdensome."

The process of creating the right account plan has been iterative for Merial. They've improved the forms, updated activities, and integrated it into their CRM system. "Before it was in our CRM system, when it was an Excel file, it was just an administrative process, and people slapped it together," Kaegi says. "Now, we've been pretty conscious about having it integrated and simple. But it all started with really taking the top reps, finding out what they were doing, and building a template for the rest of the team."

Some companies may not have strategic account plans at all, only tactical account plans. Companies that sell all products or services through a very transactional sales process, for example, might only have tactical plans. Tactical plans are good for companies with a relatively flat Pareto curve, in that the bulk of their revenue is made up of midsized accounts. For example, before Merial began focusing on large hospitals, its customers were mostly small veterinary practices and its account plans were mostly tactical. Some companies intentionally have a strategy that focuses on small business. Tactical plans are simple and short, but force the rep to think through how to achieve goals. They need to include information that makes sense for a larger number of accounts, but also prompts thinking, rather than just reacting to customers. The three major components for a tactical account plan are:

- your current position
- goals for the account
- action plan and tactics.

Aspirational Account Plan

Aspirational accounts are sometimes called "$100 million accounts" (they're covered more completely in chapter 6). But that doesn't necessarily mean the account is or will ever be worth $100 million. The point is that you're swinging for the fences. These account plans focus on game-changing growth. The aspirational account plan breaks from tradition in that it doesn't plan incrementally. Instead, it starts from a long-term goal and then works backward.

Rather than starting with your current position and building up incrementally (for example, "Let's grow this account 10 percent each year"), start with where you want to be in the account five years out—without the constraints of your current environment. Where the strategic account plan can constrain people's thinking by working step by step, the aspirational account plan allows the team to release its inhibitions and not worry about how the plan will affect its quota next year.

For example, if you go to Microsoft and say, "We want to do $100 million of business with you in the next five years," it can change the client's way of thinking about you. Even if you're not doing a fraction of that—even if you're not doing a fraction of that in any account—you position yourself in the eyes of your client differently because you're letting the client know where you want to go.

As soon as you set an audacious revenue goal and a timeframe on the aspirational account plan, it creates a trajectory. Team members suddenly understand they have to do something significant and different, such as pull in partners, hire more salespeople, or increase production. This perspective reshapes the team's expectations and broadens thinking beyond what's been done before.

Components of an aspirational account include what you can sell to the customer, how you can partner with the customer, and what you can buy from the customer to create a 360-degree partnership. Aspirational account plans have the same six basic components as the strategic account plan. The difference is perspective—start with the huge revenue goal in mind and work backward—and involves more partnerships with the customer and perhaps third parties.

Pursuit Plan

Pursuit plans are for new customers. Structurally, this is the same as the strategic account plan. But it requires more work and time to gather the information, specifically about buyers within the account. If it's an account with which you don't have any business, or if the business is very new and you have limited information, use pursuit plans rather than strategic account plans.

Pursuit plans don't contain the level of history and performance with the account that the strategic account plan contains, but focus more on learning, near-term goals, and establishing a foothold in the account. This account plan allows for a learning curve, but demands that you actively collect the information and determine the customer's needs. Once you begin winning business, the account plan becomes either a strategic plan, or, if the revenue is relatively small and the sales process transactional, a tactical plan. If there's lots of potential, it could become an aspirational plan.

When developing a pursuit plan, look for sources of information about the market and the account, which might include public information or insiders like coaches or partner companies. New accounts are always more difficult simply because you know less. But account plans are still critical to getting and growing the business. Any information you have about a new customer will allow you to be more insightful about what you can provide.

At SalesGlobe, we've had our own wins and losses, and pursuit plans have become critical for our firm. When we pursue a new account, we want to develop the proposal from the customer's perspective as much as possible. We want to move from boilerplate to customized insight. For example, a few years ago we were trying to win new business with a large media company in the automotive industry. The company had acquired several other companies and had a real need to rationalize its sales teams and go-to-market approach. From our perspective, it was a lucrative opportunity. The challenge was that we didn't know a lot about the business and there was already an incumbent—another sales effectiveness firm in place doing a separate project. We put together our pursuit plan and our pitch, but the company didn't share a lot of information. We ultimately lost the opportunity—it went to the incumbent—but it was a good lesson in doing the profile and position part of the account plan.

As you profile the account, pay attention to a few important areas that can predict your success:

- Do you know the industry?
- Do you have the subject matter expertise they're looking for?
- Do you have multiple buyer relationships or just a single point of contact?
- Are you a fit with the company in terms of where you tend to be strong? For example, if you have a strong track record with Fortune 500 companies in the insurance industry, you have a better chance than with a midcap manufacturer.
- Are you differentiated? Is what you have to say unique?
- Are you an incumbent? This is the most powerful and perhaps the hardest to overcome.

Appendix 11 illustrates a scoring matrix you can use to determine if you're positioned to win a deal. In the opportunity we didn't win, we couldn't answer yes to many of the previous questions. The matrix is helpful in identifying specific weak points that need attention in your pursuit plan. Account pursuits require investments—more so than a strategic or tactical plan in which you're retaining or developing revenue. You have to determine whether your odds are good enough to warrant the investment. Look at these factors and decide whether to make the investment.

In another example, we pursued a company where we could answer yes to most of those questions, the exception being that we were not an incumbent. It was a large staffing company, and we had spent years investing in research within that industry. We were an authority in that sector, and we had multiple buyer relationships because our research put us in contact with a lot of people in the field. The company was a Fortune 500 company, which was a good fit in terms of the complexity of issues we typically deal with. We had subject matter expertise that was enhanced through our research. Because of what we knew about the industry, we were able to offer a differentiated value proposition and won the business, while the incumbent, which had rested on the strength of its relationships, was forced out.

Effective account planning requires insight and investment. While the profile and position section of an account plan looks like homework—especially for a pursuit plan—it provides insight you need to win. Many people think they know this information, that it lives in their head. But it's probably not as accurate as you think, and the work shouldn't be done in isolation. Your team will challenge what you truly know about the account.

5 Questions to Ask About Account Plan Structure

1. What is our organization's vision around account planning?
2. What should our plans look like to achieve the right tension between execution and information?
3. Have we properly segmented accounts that warrant plans into strategic, tactical, aspirational, and pursuit?
4. Do our account tactics support clear objectives with visible actions to which the team can be held accountable?
5. Are we committed to making the account planning process a routine part of our culture?

Chapter 3

Set the Goal

I was a chubby kid at 15, which made my teenage years depressing. Because I was chubby, I was picked on in school by all the other kids (and those were my friends). I was always the last kid selected to a team for dodgeball and the first to then get violently nailed by the ball. After living like this for a while, I developed an inner drive for something better. I wanted to be bigger and stronger than the other kids. I wanted to do something great. But to do this, I knew I needed a goal and a plan.

I found my inspiration in muscle magazines. Charles Atlas, a famous bodybuilder in the early 1900s who advertised in these magazines, got to me. Weighing about 150 pounds at the time, I figured if I could bench press twice my body weight, I would feel more comfortable and confident.

Ultimately it took about three years. But over those three years, everything changed. I went from the last kid picked for the team to the first. Focused on my 300-pound bench press goal, I devoted my days to my workout plan, which included a better diet and a strict workout schedule. I started in my garage with a set of concrete-filled plastic weights from Sears. Back then, sporting goods stores didn't carry weight lifting equipment and there were few gyms outside of the weight rooms at local high schools. I saved lawn mowing money and bought a mail order set of real barbells and a bench that arrived one day in the back of a semi-truck that pulled up in front of the house. Those, and a good spotter who I worked out with, took me to the next level. I eventually moved up to working out at the Philadelphia YMCA when I was in college.

My first 300-pound lift was just a formality at that point. I was in shape, and I wasn't getting picked on anymore. But I remember it vividly. I had two 45-pound plates and a 25-pound, 10-pound, and 2.5-pound plate on each end of a 45-pound bar. When I lifted the bar from the rack with a spotter standing over me for safety, I could feel the solid steel bar actually bend. As I slowly lowered the bar to my chest, I could feel my joints creaking—not normal for an 18-year-old. I pushed through, completed the lift, and dropped the bar back into the rack.

After completing my journey, I realized two things. First, I would never have bench-pressed 300 pounds if I hadn't set that as my goal. Second, in the end, it wasn't just about the goal. It was about the learning, accomplishment, and gratification I experienced along the way. And when working with sales teams, you should not overlook this second realization. The goals your sales organization sets should factor in what the sales team can learn from its interactions with customers to enhance the account planning process and improve goal setting for future account plans.

Whether you're lifting weights, developing new skills to improve on the job, or looking to help your sales team drive revenue, you need to set goals to guide you on your path to success. Great account plans aren't that different. For an account plan to work, the sales team has to have a clear long-term goal. It has to be audacious enough to be worth your investment. And you can't just go through the motions. No pain, no gain.

Allocation of the Business Plan

At the heart of every account plan is a number, a revenue amount upon which the success or failure of the account plan hangs. So where does this number come from?

The answer, hopefully, is several places. First and foremost, it comes from the top. As part of the overall strategy of the business, the C-level, including the chief sales officer, has a revenue goal for the company. That goal is divided into revenue from current customers that the company expects to retain, and revenue from current customers to whom the company would like to sell additional products or services. And then, most likely, the company would also like to see some new customers.

This annual company revenue goal is then passed down to the sales organization, which divides it further by teams, regions, and accounts. The number is now in the form of account goals, or, from another perspective, quotas for sales teams and individual reps. In best practice sales organizations, sales leaders consider the input of sales managers and reps about which accounts (or even markets) have the most potential for new revenue and the accounts (or markets) that might be highly penetrated. There's always some tension between the C-level, finance, sales leadership, and the sales organization about sales goals and what's realistic given the actual potential in the market. There's also a tension between an aggressive account planning process and the goals that the sales organization will have to take on. Sales teams don't want to have goals they can't achieve. And if the teams do achieve those audacious goals, they don't want to be rewarded with an even higher quota the following year. If that happens, they'll probably purposefully deflate their numbers, and they might not be proponents of an account plan with aggressive growth goals.

Account plans are necessary for visibility between the C-level and the street level, says Camie Shelmire, chief client officer at Aricent. "At the executive level, account plans are needed so that a sales leader, CSO, or president can see where you are with the client business on a quarterly basis. You're accountable to the business. That's one layer. At a second layer, it's important for the account leader to have a clear plan. It's a good way for the organization to stay disciplined on the road map to achieve their revenue goal."

Retaining, Upselling or Cross-Selling, and Acquiring Accounts

At the highest level, companies have three sources of growth: retaining revenue from current customers, growing revenue from current customers, and acquiring new revenue from new customers. Each account plan is trying to develop customers to spend more by either purchasing new products or services or introducing new buyers within the same company. Each account—whether retaining, developing, or acquiring new customers—is part of that overall growth plan.

A critical part of an account plan is understanding how this revenue contributes to the company's overall growth plan. It's also important to understand the retained, developed, and new acquisition growth rates in the accounts for which you're planning. Figure 3-1 illustrates how these three sources of growth relate to one another.

For each account determine whether that revenue is:

- **Retained revenue.** Retention by definition can be at most 100 percent. For each account, determine if it has retained 100 percent of the revenue from year one or less. Anything above 100 percent is growth revenue. Tally all the retained revenue from those accounts, and divide that number by year one revenue. This is your retained rate. It's rare to retain 100 percent of revenue year over year. Therefore, to grow, you first have to recover revenue that's been churned, either through new business or by upselling or cross-selling current customers, before you can increase revenue beyond last year's.

- **Upsell and cross-sell revenue.** Next, identify your upsell and cross-sell revenue. Calculate the revenue in year two that was above or in addition to the revenue you had in year one. If an account did $100 of business in year one and $110 in year two, you'd have $100 of retention and $10 of upsell and cross-sell revenue. If an account did $100 of business with you in year one and $90 in year two, then you'd have 90 percent retained, 10 percent churned, and 0 percent upsell and cross-sell revenue. Add your upsell and cross-sell amounts and divide by year one total revenue to get your upsell and cross-sell rate.

- **New acquisition revenue.** Finally, take any accounts at the end of year two that had no revenue with your company in year one. The total revenue for those accounts is your acquisition revenue.

Figure 3-1. Sources of Growth Waterfall

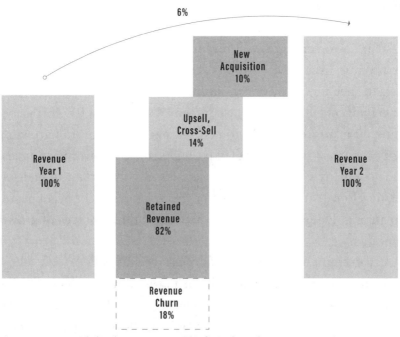

Companies don't grow in a straight line from year to year. This figure shows that a company retains some revenue from year one and it churns some revenue from year one; the company also upsells and cross-sells to current customers and acquires new revenue from new customers. All this contributes to the final year two revenue. In this example, the company churned 18 percent of its revenue between year one and year two, retaining 82 percent of its revenue. The company won 14 percent additional revenue from current customers by upselling or cross-selling to them. The company also acquired 10 percent new revenue from new customers. Overall, from year one to year two, the company grew 6 percent by retaining, upselling or cross-selling, and acquiring new revenue, even though it lost 18 percent of its year one revenue (which is not abnormal).

This analysis can help you get a baseline understanding of your retained, upsell and cross-sell, and new growth rates. In general, you have to put more resources per dollar on new account acquisition versus current account retention or upsell and cross-sell because new accounts take more work and more time to close. The odds of winning the business are often lower, and usually the size of the win is smaller. Sometimes, however, you have to accept these small wins—or even provide something for free—just to get in the door.

Most companies, on average, retain about 82 to 84 percent of their revenue year to year. They penetrate another 15 to 20 percent through upselling and cross-selling, and revenue from new customer acquisition makes up eight to 10 percent. The company's sales strategy will determine the balance between retained, upsell and cross-sell, and new account growth, and account plans should follow suit. If the company is well established in major accounts it will have more of an expectation of growth in retention and upsell and cross-sell than in new account acquisition. In general, most companies use account plans for the development of current accounts, and a pursuit plan for the acquisition of new accounts.

Cillian O'Grady, SMB EMEA sales leader at Citrix GetGo, sorts his accounts according to the type of revenue each will bring. Then, he and his team create account plans for the top existing customer accounts.

"We would look at our current install base and the penetration rates across the account," he says. "There are some customers who would use one product, and some would use multiple products. So we would identify which parts of the account were strong, and the areas that we didn't have any relationships in, or didn't have any business in. And we'd also look at which products, based on the type of customer account, that we could potentially target for upsell or cross-sell, to penetrate that account. We typically have to target different buyer personas in different departments."

The account plan should culminate in a goal build. Retention rates explain what retained revenue you expect to have in the account. The gap between retained revenue and your goal will then be the developed growth that you're going to pursue in that account.

Goal Build

I use the term *goal build* to describe the practice of listing all the possible sales opportunities that can help you achieve your sales goal. Listing the buyer, the offer, and the value of that offer clearly spells out how you might achieve this revenue goal. While most salespeople have this information floating around in their head, committing it to paper in a room with the larger sales team illustrates to everyone how close or far off the team is. More important, it forces the team to brainstorm any sales opportunities beyond the obvious low-hanging fruit. The goal build is not meant to be a precise exercise, guaranteeing closed deals; it's a discussion-based exchange of ideas, centered on known buyers, offers, and revenue, and new buyers, offers, and revenue.

A note about the difference between the goal and forecast: A forecast is a projection of what is likely to happen each quarter and is often geared toward investors. Forecasts are made as accurately as possible, but some businesses are easier to forecast than others. Those responsible for the forecast look at revenue numbers in the pipeline above a certain level of probability. Finance and sales leaders forecast next quarter's or next year's results based on what the sales team has already closed or should close, using known information and deals in the pipeline.

A company's goal is more aspirational and goes beyond the forecast. The goal is what you would like, based on the account leader's understanding of the account's needs and what she thinks she can accomplish within the account, even if it's not in the forecast.

The revenue goal for the account is the foundation for the account plan. It identifies your starting point and current state from a market perspective, a customer perspective, and your own perspective. You have booked a certain amount of known revenue in backlog, renewals, or retention. On top of the known revenue and backlog, you have new growth you plan to close. While some of it may show up in the forecast, a lot of it will truly be part of your goals and aspirations for the account. In fact, if you do it right, your goal build will be a couple of multiples of your actual goal, and will include some big opportunities that go beyond what you might think is possible (appendix 12).

The C-level sets the overall revenue goal for the company, and then each account is responsible for its own portion. The goal build identifies specific opportunities within your account that will help you reach your revenue goal.

For example, let's say the revenue goal for your account is $40 million. Adding up the retained revenue and expected renewals gives us a $12 million starting point. So, now you have to sell $28 million in new revenue. If, in your account planning goal build, you identify only $28 million in revenue, you're probably not going to make it. It's simply too short-sighted, and there's no way you can close 100 percent of your expected deals. Because best practice is to have at least 2.5 to three times your goal in the pipeline at any point in the year, push your account plan goal to have 2.5 to three times the revenue you need. If you have a strong multiple like that starting out, you'll add more as you go during the year and your odds of reaching your goal rise significantly. So, you'll need to identify at least $70 million in incremental growth opportunities in your goal build.

To hit your revenue goal of $40 million in this account, you have to identify $70 million of opportunity—and that's on top of the $12 million of retained revenue. Sounds like a lot, and it is—which is why you need to map it out.

First, list the known opportunities: the offer, the buyer, and the value. Then add up the value of these offers. You probably won't be at $70 million yet. This first step is just flushing the lines to get the obvious ideas on the table. If you did get to $70 million on the first pass, congratulations. You probably need a higher goal.

Next, it's time to put your thinking cap on. Go through each business unit, division, and department of the account, as well as each potential buyer, and ask, "What do they need?" Refer to your needs map (section 2 of your account plan) and identify what you can do for them to add value. Go around the room with the team and brainstorm. At the end of this round, ask one more question: "What really big opportunities, worth at least $10 million or $15 million each, have we not yet thought of or do we think we're not ready to put down on paper?" Add those in and you should be at $70 million or more.

This may sound difficult, but we've seen it in action, and it's incredible what opportunities emerge. We did this exact exercise with a technology company last year. The accounts were large, so this particular team was writing an account plan for one account we'll call ABC. The sales team had done its homework and completed the profile and position section of the account plan before the meeting. The team had learned that ABC's total budget for this type of service was $2.9 billion—a huge number, indicating a lot of potential.

Their goal for this account was $52 million, including $32 million of expected retained revenue. Our client wanted to increase the account by $20 million. Therefore, the team needed to put 2.5 times that in the pipeline, or $50 million. I remember standing at the front of the conference room in New York, working through this exercise. I stood in front of the flipchart, and announced that we were going to list $50 million worth of new work with this account, excluding the $32 million in retained revenue. Their reactions ranged from puzzled to weary to incredulous. But we persevered, and slowly, the ideas came. We identified five different projects that were worth an estimated $2 million each. At first those $2 million projects felt like drops in a bucket, but finding five of them made the $50 million number suddenly feel more achievable.

We thought some more, ate some pastries, and came up with a $4 million project, two $6 million projects, a $10 million project, and a $14 million project. Within a few hours—before lunch, even—the team members had identified $50 million of potential work with the client that, they admitted, they would not have considered if they had not walked through the goal build exercise. They would have considered opportunities throughout the year, and certainly tried to meet the original $50 million goal. But the account planning session forced them to specify potential buyers and projects. Once the opportunities were identified, they became part of section 4, or the action plan, in which specific actions were listed to make sure each opportunity became a reality.

At LexisNexis, account planning sessions include a similar goal building exercise so the sales teams can determine how to achieve their target numbers for each account.

"A big part of the account plan is the opportunities," says David Long, vice president of strategic sales. "We ask, 'What's in the pipeline? What deals are in motion? What are the deals that have recently closed and the revenue is not yet recognized? What is the current financial state of the account?' It's all built into the financial component of the plan. That's why it's got to be a living, breathing document, because all of those things that influence the financials are ever changing. They've got to continue to be updated and revised."

5 Questions to Ask About Building Your Goal

1. How has the account grown historically between retention and upselling or cross-selling, and where are the opportunities to improve those growth rates?
2. Have you separated the conversation about setting the growth goal for the account from setting quotas so that the sales team can think aspirationally?
3. Are you setting your expectations for growth of the account high enough?
4. Have you found at least 2.5 times your incremental growth goal in opportunities?
5. Have you identified several big deals as part of your goal build?

Chapter 4

Create the Habits

Several years ago, I worked with a communications hardware company on its account planning strategy. It was not the company's first attempt at account planning, nor its second or third. This company had tried and failed to establish an account planning practice for nearly a decade.

This was a company of engineers, and its biggest problem was that they were too smart. Each time the account planning process was announced, individual teams began to tweak the documents, the process, and the communications. Almost everyone offered "improvements," and the end result was an account plan that was so involved no one had time to complete it. And I heard more than a few complaints from leaders that they couldn't follow the plans because of their complexity. So, they fell to the wayside.

When I arrived, my questions about a new account planning process were answered with eye rolls or deep groans. I heard, "Here we go again," and, "This will never last." The sales organization believed this would be yet another difficult exercise that wouldn't get off the ground. But it did. We simplified the plan documents and the process, and we made them uniform. That was the value. All the account teams could settle their minds because they had a simple process to follow, and an emphasis was placed on consistency in the plans across teams. The leaders wanted the same components in the same order so they didn't have to reorient themselves to each plan. And although they hadn't realized they were burdening themselves by complicating the process at the time, this news came as a relief to the sales teams. They didn't have to go through all the machinations of trying to come up with a brilliant account plan; in fact, they were asked not to. Just follow the process.

The simpler account planning process allowed sales managers to get a better view of the past, present, and future of each account. They could compare strategies between accounts and make better critiques and recommendations to the teams because they could actually understand the plans. The account plans became easier to coach, and accountability for the actions increased. The organization knew the process was working after about 12 months, when they realized they had been using the process and updating the plans during the year and then actually jumped into the annual cycle again without the typical rethinking and redesigning that had hindered the process in prior years.

The real accomplishment was getting the right people—including people on the marketing, delivery, and sales operations teams—to make account planning part of their regular cadence of activity. They had made it a habit.

This chapter outlines the four critical habits I see in teams that have achieved long-term account planning success: think before you plan, motivate and reward the teams, establish a cycle, and demand accountability. Making habits out of these four concepts is not easy, and will take time and perhaps a change management process. But the point of creating habits is that you don't have to do the hard work of starting over year after year. Instead, devote that time and energy to building the following habits, and work toward making account planning a respected and vital practice.

Habit 1: Think Before You Plan

At SalesGlobe, we do a lot of work designing sales compensation programs. It happens all the time, but it never fails to surprise me: We'll go into our first meeting to discuss ideas for new incentive plans, and people have their spreadsheets and calculators set out. They're ready to jump into the mechanics of the plan—base pay versus incentive pay, threshold levels and upside limits, mechanics and accelerators. They're like teenagers who want to start altering the transmission and fuel injectors of the car before they even know if they need a car to get where they're going. It sounds basic but it's a major point: You have to know what you want the salespeople to do before you can figure out how to motivate them to do it. You need a sales strategy and clearly defined sales roles so salespeople are not running into one another and wasting energy and money doing all the wrong things.

The same is true with account planning. Teams want to dive into the template and open up their CRM system to look at potential deals. But the first habit to master is strategic thinking. Teams have to get out of the habit of jumping into the plan document and into the habit of discussing where they want to go with the account. It's easy to get caught up in the tools and technology, but those are just support elements. The real account planning is the thinking that happens when a team sits down to discuss how to solve problems for the customer. First and foremost, you're trying to accomplish a goal: How can you grow 20 percent (or 500 percent if it's aspirational) in this account? How do you retain your revenue? How do your expand in certain product groups?

"I always told my salespeople that account planning is figuring out how to think critically and how to communicate well," says John Dupree, partner at investment firm Opus Faveo Innovation Development and former senior vice president of business sales at Sprint. "With account planning, the actual information is going to change from quarter to quarter, year to year. The thinking process is what's great about account planning.

"What you want at the end of the day," Dupree continues, "is not someone who knows every bit of information about that customer. You want someone that knows enough about that customer that he can then turn around and look at your company through that customer's eyes, and see where there's opportunity. And that's a hugely different thing."

During his time at Sprint, Dupree estimates that between 50 and 60 percent of his salespeople knew every bit of information about the customer, but only 10 or 15 percent could see Sprint from their customer's eyes. But he could immediately identify those sales reps because they spoke confidently about what was going on in the customer's business, how the customer perceived Sprint, and where the customer sensed value. "It was impressive when someone looked at this as a process of thinking and communicating, not as an accumulation of information," he says. "It's a big distinction. It has a lot to do with the habits and discipline, critical thinking, and communication."

Account planning is not about filling in the boxes, but about problem solving for the account. The account plan becomes the enabler. It's important for the account teams to understand this: The mindset that the account plan facilitates is what helps the account grow. If you're jumping into your account planning tools and templates and haven't gone through the steps of asking the right questions about the account with your team, you're getting ahead of yourself. Break this habit and replace it with discussions, confirmation of strategy, and innovative thinking.

Habit 2: Motivate and Reward the Teams

One of the biggest reasons companies fail at account planning is that sales teams don't want to do it. They're not motivated. So, for account planning to become a habit, you need to include motivating factors and rewards.

"Salespeople are wonderfully efficient economic engines," says Dupree. "If they don't consider it a priority, they're not going to spend the time to do it." Dupree says that at Sprint, account planning (through its customer-centric Discovery program) was a highly regarded, celebrated activity. "That program was one of our most lauded, and it served as evidence to the rest of the company that only the best people could go through that program."

In my experience, the biggest motivators for salespeople are:

- **Incentive pay.** Incentive pay is a direct financial reward for being successful in sales. Typically, it's a commission or bonus tied to sales results. Sales leaders tend to like sales organizations that are motivated by incentives because they know how to focus them. They'll follow the money. If a salesperson makes the connection that doing great account planning ultimately results in great incentive pay, she may be motivated to do great account planning.

- **Recognition in the organization.** The popular view about salespeople is that they're coin-operated and only motivated by money. But that's not true. Most salespeople are also highly motivated by recognition, which usually refers to the salesperson's peers and leadership. Incentive pay is great, but recognition on top of incentive pay can sweeten the deal. President's Club trips usually wield a lot of power because they're elite: Everyone knows who's going and who's not, and often the rep's significant other is invited as well, extending the recognition even further to his personal life. Recognizing reps for successful account strategies and plans that produce results can motivate them to establish the habit.

- **Winning the deal.** Salespeople crave a win. It's closely related to recognition, but winning the deal also has to do with personal satisfaction. Winning provides a sense of accomplishment, offers bragging rights in the organization, and elevates the salesperson's position in the company. Think about the last time a rep closed a major deal with a big customer that was highly valued by the organization. It was a great accomplishment and motivator for the rep. It was also a big motivator for the other salespeople because they probably saw the possibility that they could do the same with other high-profile accounts. If winning the deal is a motivator in your organization, connect account planning to increase the odds of landing those big deals.

- **Meeting a customer need.** Being appreciated by the customer for great work, for solving a difficult problem, or for making life better for the customer is motivational for any rep. We all love to be complimented for a job well done, no matter how much you see it as just doing the right thing. Great account planning is directly related to meeting customer needs and making customers successful. If meeting customer needs is motivational to your reps, it's a clear link to account planning.

To make account planning a habit, sales leaders and sales enablers have to tie it to one or more of these motivating factors.

Initially, the team can be motivated by its leaders. Leadership sets the expectation that everyone is going to participate in account planning. This type of directive is necessary for the beginning of the account planning program and at certain checkpoints throughout the year. But constant direction from leadership can only last so long. Sales leaders have to find a way to motivate the sales organization to run account planning tactics itself. But by helping to get the program started, sales enablers will create success in the form of increased connections with the customer, increased visibility to the customer's problems, and eventually, increased wins. Wins are the type of reward that motivates the team to stick with account planning. And once salespeople start to see those rewards, they can then start to create the habit of account planning.

Be forewarned, however, that success creates another risk: complacency. Reps begin to think, "We don't need to do account planning anymore because we're doing so well," and they start to let up on the process. The more success a rep has, often the less desire he has for additional success. Reps tend to reach a point of financial satisfaction in which pushing harder isn't worth the incremental dollars that come with it. Economists call it the law of marginal utility and often use the example of a chocolate chip cookie. If you're really hungry for a chocolate chip cookie, you might be willing to pay a lot of money for one—maybe $3. You might be willing to pay a lot of money for the second one, too. But as your cookie craving is satisfied, the amount you're willing to pay for another diminishes. You probably wouldn't pay $3 for a third cookie, maybe just $1. You'd be willing to pay even less for a sixth because you'd probably no longer want it.

The same principle applies here. Salespeople who earn plenty of money eventually hit their level of diminishing marginal utility. They don't want to continue to push harder to get that extra dollar because the extra effort is not worth it. Success at account planning then can dull your desire to continue adhering to the habit because you think you don't have to. At this point, leadership has to say, "I don't care how you feel about it; you have to continue the discipline of doing it."

It's a dangerous cycle: The pipeline dries up and creates an urgency to get account planning under way. And then, once that works, there's less urgency to stick to the planning. So sales goes back to business as usual, which does not include a regular account planning process. They start to coast.

"Account planning drives demand and takes some of the pressure off of the pipeline, and then people get busy, and then they're too busy to plan. It becomes a cycle over the long term—you're not planning, and then the market turns, and things start to dry up again, and you start going back in that cycle," says Brad Kaegi, head of marketing for the Pets EMEA region at Merial.

Sprint had account planning meetings twice a year, and it was "an incredible amount of work," says Dupree. So, they made sure sales teams were presenting to senior leaders, who were also taking a full day to listen to the plans. Involving the valuable time of leadership, he says, sent a message to all 3,000 salespeople that knowing your customer and having a plan was vitally important. "Because we, from John Dupree and down, spent a lot of our time listening to these account plans," he says.

And it worked. Relatively quickly, account planning became a process that was important culturally. Salespeople began to tell Dupree that they worked hard at account planning because he had asked them to, and because he and other senior leaders took the time to listen to the plans and respond to them: "It elevated the importance of doing account planning."

In the case of complex accounts, to show that account planning was in their interest, Dupree kept a running quarterly comparison between the accounts that did extensive account planning with the customer and the accounts that did no planning. "We saw that the planning had a huge impact," he says. The accounts with extensive planning came in multiple tens of percentage points ahead in revenue penetration and revenue growth.

"Account planning just fundamentally makes a difference," Dupree continues. "You're always going to have people who just don't believe it, who think that they're so good they don't need it, or they just don't care. But those people ultimately cycle out of the business—unless they are absolutely so gifted that they can do it without a plan. But I've rarely seen those types of people."

Habit 3: Establish the Cycle

So what's the right schedule of events to keep the plan alive beyond that first meeting? The answer depends on your sales organization. Typically, sales organizations try to accomplish a lot at the beginning of the year, including sales kick-off meetings, strategy discussions, training, and sales compensation and quota communications. There's no way to do it all at once.

Ideally, account planning will fit within a company's strategic planning cycle. For a company in a fiscal year, it probably needs to start in the third quarter so people can work on the plans and continue their day jobs. This staggers the amount of nonselling work that teams have to do. It also ensures those plans are firmly in place at the beginning of the year. (You don't want account planning to become a fire drill or a process you have to shortcut. The tyranny of the urgent will always overtake account planning, so you have to allow enough time for both.) And, ideally, once the process gets going, the account plans are refreshed each year, rather than started from scratch. After the first year, the account planning process is largely about updating the prior version and ensuring the right people contribute and buy into it.

LexisNexis holds large account planning meetings once a year, with two updates throughout the year. "We try to keep it so that it's not a one-time event, but it's a living, breathing document and process that we continue to update and gather feedback, and alter as the year goes on," says David Long, vice president of strategic sales. Ask for and inspect updates and accountabilities frequently. Plans require adjustment throughout the year as tactics are attempted and conditions evolve.

Much of the plan's success is driven by the level of participation and engagement from all contributing parties. That can be a challenge, especially for an annual in-person meeting. Kaegi and his team would attempt to get the account team, marketing, product development, and leadership in a room to present and refine the account plan. "But, we quickly found out that trying to find a day to get on everybody's calendar to do that was simply not feasible," he says. "We do almost 50 account plans. It takes a lot of time and planning, and the demand on the supporting organizations was pretty significant."

Getting dozens of key people to an account planning meeting once or twice a year can be a challenge, but keeping the account plan alive and relevant is critical. Maintaining a regular cadence of meetings and touch-points to assess the account's health and the accuracy of the account plan keeps it alive throughout the year and creates a reliable method of tracking and predicting growth in that account year after year. "I would argue that if you had good adherence to a planning process, and you focused and thought about it, everything could be organized a little better," says Kaegi.

You should aim for in-person meetings, rather than relying on web conferences or phone calls. The team chemistry and idea-sharing is almost impossible to replicate over the phone. When at all possible, challenges of cost and time should take a backseat to the benefits of in-person meetings, even if they are infinitely more difficult to pull off.

"Everybody knows account planning is important, but our biggest challenge is scheduling," says David Long. "Everybody wants to be involved, because they want a saddle to success; they want to contribute to our client strategies. But they have day jobs. We would love to block off three weeks where no one did anything other than build and support account planning. But that's just not reality. Ultimately, we have to do more by telephone, and it just stinks because you know people are multitasking." In the end, do what needs to be done to get people talking about the account plan and to keep the conversation rolling.

I've witnessed many sales organizations run into barriers, such as scheduling, and drop the whole thing rather than work through problems. It's easier to ignore account planning, and it's culturally acceptable because so many organizations do. My team and I recently worked with a global marketing firm that struggled to establish a living account planning process. The account leader told me, "There's zero commitment to this process. Even if we create account plans, we ignore them. In the end, we get business by responding to RFPs, and that keeps us busy enough." The account leader wasn't against a new process; he just didn't have any faith that the leadership would demand follow-through.

What he said was true. The sales leadership in this company didn't proactively target accounts because there were too many to go after. They didn't segment or prioritize potential customers (by industry, by product match, by strategic fit), and because of the breadth of their products and services, almost any company was a potential customer. They were overwhelmed and paralyzed. So their "sales process" was to wait for RFPs. It's a dangerous strategy. While seemingly easier because the opportunity is clearly identified, the odds of winning a deal born from an RFP are lower because it's competitive. The company was far better off targeting customers and proactively selling to them, with a plan of course. Once they saw the value of proactive plans, the sales organization began the work and saw results. And that inspired new habits.

No matter the exact cadence of meetings, management has to take the time to regularly review the account plans. "The key to making account planning a living process is management review," says Jill Merken, vice president of global sales operations and inside sales at Gemalto, a global digital services company. "I have seen it done very well. Every quarter, at a quarterly business review, my team of sales vice presidents and I would review eight to 10 account plans. And then, when there was a deal or an opportunity on those, we would look to see how it matched against the quarterly account plan.

"In between management reviews, the account leaders would ask, 'OK, what are we doing in this account? How well are we doing?' because they were managed by it," she continues. "And at the end of the year, each sales manager would have to give the sales VP an update: 'I have eight accounts in my region; here is the status of those accounts. We're growing it, we're not growing it, we've got a footprint here, we're trying to get in here.' Having these reviews created accountability to keep the team moving, but really it comes down to management thinking this process is important. If it's not important to management, then why should a rep spend the time doing it?"

One final note about establishing a cycle: Take the time to introduce account planning properly, whether it's a new or updated program in your company. One of the biggest mistakes I see in a new account planning program is a rushed roll-out. Kaegi saw this happen at Merial: "In the early days of account planning at Merial, they wanted to roll it out to everyone without any testing. And it failed, because they hadn't piloted it. The temptation was to just do the whole thing at once instead of piloting it and making sure that they could roll it out in stages and do it correctly."

Consider pilot programs with select accounts to find out what works and what doesn't for your organization, listen to the feedback of the sales teams, and make any adjustments necessary. Once other sales teams see their peers' success with account planning, they might be less resistant when it's time for them to add a cycle of account planning to their habits.

Habit 4: Demand Accountability

If no one holds the sales teams accountable for plan presentations or status updates on the action items, the message is clear: Account planning is a one-time exercise that can be ignored for the rest of the year. And the teams will return to their normal activities.

Three factors I've found effective for accountability are direction, leadership demonstration, and measurement. First, give clear direction on the account plan strategy and process and set the expectation that the team will follow. Before the annual account planning meeting is finished, make sure team members clearly understand their commitments and have an accountability point (a deliverable at a target date). Hold people responsible for those commitments.

Second, leadership should demonstrate the account planning process in action and make it the system of record. This means the chief sales officer and sales leaders must actually use the account plans in their conversations with the team. When a sales leader visits a salesperson in her city and goes on account visits, the sales leader needs to ask for the account plan and use it to get up to speed on the account. No account plan, no customer visit. Gone are the days of asking about the account on the car ride over. If the reps know the leaders are using the account plans, they will too.

"Our account plans are used by the executives," says Merken. "If an executive is going to visit a customer, there is an executive briefing document created by the account team. It's maybe 10 questions." The rep has to do some research, including calling the client services group or other internal functions, and understand: Have there been any technical issues with this client? Do we have any returns? Are there any products that aren't working? Is there any kind of news brief? Anything published regarding the company's financials? Any major executive changes? Then, says Merken, there is always a 30-minute call between that executive, the rep, and their managers to go through the briefing document so that the executive will know what he is walking into. "At first, there was a lot of grumbling," says Merken, "but it helps everyone."

Also, while sales leaders run account planning, it can't be seen as a sales-only program. In a multifunctional team, the accountability must be driven by the leaders of those functions: leaders of the marketing team, finance team, and operations team. These leaders have to see account planning as a critical, cross-functional process in the organization. The CSO has to enlist the leaders into her vision of account planning and why it's critical for them to be part of it. If she can't do it, she'll have to go up to the next level—to the president of the company—to rope everyone in.

Third, measure and recognize performance relative to the account plans. Measure and recognize great account strategies. Measure and recognize sales results by making the connection to how the account plan drove those results. Measure and recognize successful account planning in the employee performance review process. It's not adequate to measure sales performance alone without measuring how the rep got there. That would be like a basketball coach only measuring the team's total score without measuring their shooting percentage, turnovers, or assists. The team may have won the game, but it may have won through sloppy play, poor teamwork, and hotdog players making most of the points independently. If you treat account planning the same way, you may win some deals, but you're not developing a repeatable system and game plan to predictably win over time. Creating accountability is a critical step in making account planning a habit.

While motivation is usually driven by the carrot, accountability tends to require a stick. The leaders of functions involved in account planning beyond sales may have to be held accountable for their role in the effectiveness of the account planning process as part of their performance evaluations. Operations and finance people should have the effectiveness of their role in account planning as one of their key performance indicators. This helps reinforce that account planning is everyone's job.

Implementing accountability sets you up well for when you're faced with a lack of compliance. It allows you to bring the hammer down. You never want to fire someone for not being part of the account planning process, but if account planning is an important enough part of the company's business processes, it has to be taken seriously. Determine your policy for lack of compliance around account planning. As I mentioned earlier, sales results alone don't give sales teams a pass on account planning. If you treat account planning compliance casually, expect casual results. Establish and maintain effective account planning habits to increase the odds of consistent account growth.

5 Questions to Ask About Creating the Habits

1. What motivates your team and how can you connect account planning to those motivators?
2. Is your team too focused on account planning tools and technology to the detriment of thinking and problem solving?
3. Are your account plans and processes overengineered or simple and straightforward?
4. What is your living account planning process and how will you keep it alive?
5. How will you create accountability for account planning, and what actions will you take for noncompliance?

Chapter 5

Understand the
Politics

In a large, open office in Manhattan, my team and I stood in the lobby waiting for Cindy. We were on the second story of a former warehouse, facing a wall of floor to ceiling windows. Light flooded in and created a silhouette as she strode toward us, a dark shape with loudly clicking heels. "Cindy," she said, thrusting out her hand. Her grip was painful, and I tried to rub feeling back into my palm as she led us to the conference room. She opened the door, greeted Kevin, the head of sales, who was already seated at the table, and briskly left.

Cindy was the head of the account management group at a large technology services company. We were hired to help create an account planning program, but, as we discovered on that first day, our job was really to mediate between sales and account management.

We had already met Kevin, a portly, astute, good-humored sales executive. As we waited for others to arrive, he offered his perspective on the company and the conflict between account management and sales. "We're a service-oriented, rather than sales-oriented, company," he began. The account managers—the people in Cindy's group—controlled the accounts. Many had worked with the same clients for years, and in some cases decades. Cindy herself had been there for almost 40 years. Her group had huge amounts of recurring revenue, but as sales began to decline, the CEO hired Kevin and a strategic sales team. They brought in new high-tech offers and launched new marketing and social media programs. "These guys know how to sell," said Kevin.

Early on, however, sales started running into opposition from account management, who wouldn't let them do their jobs. "Account management is blocking us out of the accounts," he told us. The account management team argued that they uniquely understood the needs of the account and that servicing the accounts well was the key to growing them. Sales was allowed into the account only if the current manager didn't feel threatened.

But account management didn't really sell; they were too busy servicing. Sales was a five-letter word to them. "We're trying to sell new business," said Kevin, "and create new accounts. But the account managers are not penetrating the accounts they currently have. They're just babysitting. There's so much opportunity, but we're not allowed in."

Cindy, it turned out, was the chief barrier. She inherently didn't understand sales. Because this was essentially the only company she had ever worked in, she didn't appreciate the way sales organizations operate. In fact, she told the CEO point-blank that she didn't know why they needed a sales organization at all. Cindy controlled a lot of revenue and when she talked, the CEO usually listened. From her perspective, the account management team worked with the clients and that was the only type of sales they needed.

"My people are pretty advanced," said Kevin. "They understand our industries and offers better than the account management people; they are better at recognizing opportunities. And they can get to C-level people at the customer. The account managers are stuck at the middle buyer level and don't have the gravitas to have meaningful conversations with leadership."

It wasn't good for business. A week before I arrived, the sales organization was fighting with account management over control of a large financial services client. Sales saw opportunities to expand the account. But the account manager had told sales, "We'll let you know when it's time to come in. We'll let you know if any new opportunities come up." In the meantime, a competitor came in, proposed a deal, and stole the business. We discovered that this feud had been raging for years. It was a slow poison drip into the company's culture.

The next day we met separately with Cindy, whose perspective was that Kevin's people were disruptive and trying to edge their way into the accounts. "Don't get me wrong," she said. "I don't mind a salesperson coming in to the account. But I don't want them sounding like a salesperson." She feared the salespeople would scare the client and ruin the relationship. She had a misperception of salespeople, and she couldn't make a distinction between a stereotypical salesperson and a seasoned sales professional, which is what Kevin had.

When we got into the account planning conversation, I asked Cindy a foundational question: "Who owns the account plan?"

She lurched across the desk. "Did Kevin tell you to ask me that?" It was obviously a point of contention. As tough and competitive as Cindy was, she knew her people were not skilled to sell. They considered their own sales organization their competitors and were protecting accounts from them, which instead helped the real competitors steal business.

It was one of the most politically charged environments I had ever witnessed, and I've seen many. These were seemingly normal people, until they began interacting with one another. But this level of misconduct hadn't appeared overnight. It had built up over the years because leadership tolerated bad behavior. People were clamoring for what they perceived to be scarce opportunities, and a culture of paranoia thrived.

What Creates Politics?

Why do companies have these types of politics? Clearly, some organizations are more political than others, resulting in rampant conflict. In an open market we call it competition. Companies compete with one another, and that's usually healthy. But politics is the ugly stepsibling to competition. When people within the same company get political, it's detrimental to the company's success. Four conditions contribute to a political environment: scarcity, lack of leadership, culture, and hyper-accountability.

Scarcity

If the company doesn't have a strong sales strategy, methodology, or sellers, then it operates in an environment of perceived scarcity rather than abundance. One of the main problems the technology services company at the beginning of the chapter dealt with was a perceived scarcity of accounts. While they had a lot of recurring revenue, they didn't have many new accounts coming in, so each account manager held tightly to what she had, protecting it from the sales organization. It was an absurd notion, but many account managers believed that if they allowed a salesperson access to their account, they would lose control of the business and therefore their job.

In fact, just the opposite was true. One of the days we were working there, we saw a woman frantically walking through the sales offices, looking for someone to help her. She had managed a $30 million account for years, and unbeknownst to her, the customer had put the business out to bid. She learned that her account was in jeopardy not through the relationships she thought she had, but when she received a general RFP sent by email. She had been so deep in servicing the account that she hadn't considered business development. She had assumed the future would look just like the past, and she had obviously missed something somewhere.

She didn't have the skills to respond to the RFP, nor had she bothered to cultivate relationships with any salespeople at her own company. On the contrary, she had spent years shutting them out. So she was in a pickle. She eventually found a salesperson, but he was in the wrong vertical—high tech, rather than insurance. He was able to help her at a high level, but between the two of them, the business was at risk. If she lost the account, chances were good that she would lose her job.

Many of the people in account management shared her beliefs: opportunities were scarce and needed to be protected.

Lack of Clear Leadership

Another driver of infighting is a lack of clear leadership. If a company is left to its own devices and has groups that are relatively equal in power, you'll probably see more politics and bickering. A strong leader will set the agenda, make clear decisions, and not tolerate deviance from those decisions. Strong leadership reduces politics.

When I began working with this company, Kevin and Cindy were each working separately with the CEO trying to implement their own strategies. Kevin wanted to define roles and ownership of opportunities, and clearly spell out how sales, account management, and the client worked together. Cindy wanted sales to stay out of account management and focus only on bringing new deals in, and then hand them over to account management.

To my utter amazement, both were fully confident that the CEO, Frank, was implementing their plan without consulting their rival. When Kevin spoke to us, he presumed the new organization structure he had proposed to the CEO was a done deal. "I already spoke with Frank. We're ready to move ahead with the new structure," he said. There was no mention of Cindy. What had she said? "I have no idea," Kevin said. "Frank said he would take care of her reaction."

This level of misconduct came from the top. Frank, a soft-spoken intellectual man, was making a bad situation worse. He was unwilling to make clear decisions about account ownership because he didn't like conflict. Frank agreed with Kevin when he talked to Kevin and agreed with Cindy when he talked to Cindy. It was a ridiculous situation.

Culture

Culture can be an enabler of politics. If you have an environment of scarcity or weak leadership, a strong culture can counter that to some degree. A culture centered on values including respect, open communication, and humility will not tolerate overly political behavior. A Machiavellian culture, however, will encourage politics and survivor-like allegiances. Where people see opportunities to take advantage of the system, their actions can feed the politics.

Hyper-Accountability

Extreme accountability—and its opposite, avoidance of accountability—can lead to political behavior. In an environment that seeks out causes for everything that happens, good or bad, extreme accountability can lead to witch hunts. "We didn't hit our numbers. Who missed their quotas, and how far off were they? We lost the ACME opportunity. What happened? Who was on the pursuit team? We invested a ton of money in developing that new idea. Why didn't it work? Who was on the development team?" An organization that seeks blame drives politics. In today's environment of fast-cycle experimentation and fast-fail development, a culture of blame can suck the life out of creativity and productivity.

The technology company in the example is not alone with its conflicts. "We see that a lot in Lexmark with our hardware management services offerings," says Sue Holub, vice president of enterprise software marketing. "The salespeople tend to align toward IT and procurement as their primary point of contact, whereas in the enterprise software realm, we see a concentration around finance and the different lines of business. So, the same account has very different entry points to move the business forward."

The account plans require multiple groups to provide input, and because of the political nature, sales is forced to reposition the offer before asking a particular group for input, says Holub. "How do we want to position the offering? How do we want to position our capability? How do we want to differentiate from competition?"

Lexmark's solution is increased communication. "We connect sales and marketing together. They have important conversations during the account plan development. There have to be a number of touch-points between different groups—sales leaders, senior management, solutions, operations—that would inform a thoughtful account plan. Each group has to ask, 'What do I want to accomplish in the account this year? What am I building toward?'" she says. The more the groups communicate, the less political the conversations become.

Effective account plans eliminate the scarcity, scrambling, and overlapping roles. Account plans create a clarity of action and mitigate the dynamics that contribute to politics and squabbling.

Understanding Roles

One of my first recommendations to defuse political situations is to understand other perspectives and priorities, and where the work of others might intersect with yours. You might not agree with everyone all the time, but understanding helps people reach across lines and work together toward a larger common goal. Wherever possible in your organization, clearly define roles, keep people in their own lanes, and establish rules of engagement with other functions. Here are the roles most vital to the account planning process and their priorities.

CSO

The CSO's main concern is always the revenue number he has to hit. It's almost always bigger than last year's number, and it usually feels unattainable. Secondarily, he's concerned with hiring and retaining the right people. Account plans help him with both.

The CSO takes requirements and feedback from rest of the C-level about where the business needs to go. He gets input from the CEO and the board of directors, who determine where the company is headed long term and near term. The CSO also gets insight from finance, led by the chief financial officer, about revenue and profitability goals, and from the chief marketing officer (CMO) about priorities for the company's products, services, and overall value proposition. For example, are there strategic products that need to be sold? Are there new products that are going to be introduced? Does the company need to change the way it's positioning to the market? The CMO and marketing also determine what market segments the organization will target. Finally, the chief people officer may have input into how the organization is building out talent and how it can support the overall account planning process.

Ultimately, the CSO's role is to give the mandate for account planning and maintain accountability. He provides insight, challenges the validity of the account plan, and confirms that the plan meets the strategy and the quota requirements.

Account Leader

At the account level, the account leader owns the account vision, objectives, and strategy to achieve those objectives. The account leader is the person who is ultimately responsible for achieving the sales goal in the account. She may be a global account manager, a national account manager, a strategic account manager, or similar. The account leader takes the account planning process and applies it to her customers. She is the owner of the process, which means she has to round up and organize the account planning team in sales and other related functions like operations, marketing, and finance, which can be a challenge. Whether the account plan succeeds or fails is determined by the account leader.

Sales Team

The sales team comprises the people who work on the account and who have responsibility for executing the account plan. These may be salespeople who cover certain business units in the account, certain product or service offers, or certain geographies. When the account goal is set, the sales team will own the entire goal, and some individual reps may own specific parts of the goal as well. For example, the account may have a $32 million goal for the year, and a regional account manager may personally carry $10 million of that goal. But because she will also get credit for the attainment of the overall $32 million, she must collaborate with the whole team, beyond her region.

Sales Enablement

Sales operations, trainers, and coaches play critical roles in the account planning process. Sales enablement may have a role in coaching, talent selection, training, incentive compensation design, and sales tool design. Sales enablement should be involved in the account planning process to ensure that the organization can fulfill the value proposition and meet the customer's budget and timing requirements.

For large strategic accounts or accounts with highly specific needs, the company may enlist the help of the product organization to develop solutions for the customer. Sometimes these specialized products and services can be spun off to other accounts in the organization.

Two important areas of marketing support include product marketing, which can help with the development or customization of the value proposition, and field marketing support, which can enable the sales team with marketing tools and special offers. Marketing can also provide somethings of value, or SOVs, including research that would be helpful to the customer, or admission to an event like a conference or industry forum, where the customer can engage with other organizations or learn about important topics.

"At Lexmark, sales and marketing coordinate around the concept of segmentation, message, and offer," says Holub. "Both at the macro level and within the account, figuring out what the right messages are to each buyer and orienting offers or content to those various roles for awareness and engagement—that's where marketing can play the strongest role. Segmentation looks at the makeup of accounts based on geography, departments, or roles. That allows you to really home in on where your sweetest spot is. And, depending on your company's enterprise account planning approach, there could be multiple sweet spots. That's where marketing has to get kind of microtactical, because you're essentially creating campaigns and programs to target one specific person with a set of messages and an offer to try and drive a specific solution forward. But that might be completely inappropriate for another person."

As in the case with Lexmark, increased communication can defuse political behavior. David Long, vice president of strategic sales at LexisNexis, describes a three-legged stool of sales, market planning, and product development. "Those three areas have to be completely aligned with not only maintaining the existing business, but also creating solutions that will drive that relationship forward. Those are really the three primary areas that construct the plan." If these three groups don't communicate successfully with one another, not only will they fail to create effective account plans, they won't be in position to respond to rapidly changing market conditions.

"The market is moving so quickly, and while our product pipeline is good and is appropriate, things change," says Long. "And when the market changes, we all have to be aligned, so our product development teams can shift swiftly to be more effective, to provide more effective solutions to the market. They get locked-in on development efforts, and, understandably, they like to know at the beginning of the year what they have to accomplish. They have road maps in place to deliver certain products or enhancements. So when the market shifts, sales has to go to them and say, 'Here's a functionality with a given solution that's really critical for a client.' That can really break their stride. And stepping into a different path, while at the same time trying to accomplish the things that they were already set to accomplish, is very challenging." The communication and relationships between sales, market planning, and product development have to be healthy for all three groups to be successful.

"It's critical to get past that inflection point where everybody is comfortable, and say, 'I don't have the answers. Let's start really thinking.' We're using our account planning sessions as real workshops to do that," he continues. "And that energizes salespeople like nothing else when others start contributing in that way."

These massive accounts require people who understand not only the features and benefits of the products and how they fit within the account, but also the operational requirements and resources the team needs to fulfill the offer. Respect for one another's role, priorities, and limits can help keep lanes clear of conflict. When leadership can clearly communicate these roles, and prevent poaching or blame, it's setting the stage for healthy account planning and collaborative teams.

Getting Over the Hurdles

For all the time wasted on political fighting, you'd think company leadership would never let this behavior continue past several hours. Unfortunately, most of us have been in environments where political behavior goes on for years, slowing progress and dragging down morale. If your sales organization is one where leadership appears content to keep the status quo, fear not. With the help of one or two reasonable colleagues, you might be able to work around those who are unable to compromise. I've seen the following four tactics help sales teams succeed when conventional interactions have failed.

Take a Perspective of Abundance Rather Than Scarcity

Help the sales team develop a mindset around the opportunities in the account rather than the limits of what it has now. Consider ways it can grow the account rather than protecting it from others in the organization. A great account planning process can help sales teams see and plan for abundance rather than squabble over scarcity. The process gives you the capability and tools to chart your destiny rather than react to the fearful attitude of others.

Recognize That You Have More Control Than You Think

At the technology services company described earlier in this chapter, despite the fact that they had organizational problems with the leaders above them, the teams found ways to make it work. For example, in the pharmaceuticals vertical they found common ground and set up collaborative teams. They didn't rely on leadership in the organization to give them cues on how they should act; they decided to be proactive. They grew their accounts and their incentive pay. While some were sucked into the vortex of politics, often using it as an excuse, others figured out how to work together and crossed organizational lines. Set up a ring of collaboration outside of politics and take control.

Increase Communication With the People You Can

A lack of communication and withholding information are currencies of politics. Information is power, and when sales teams open up communications with the people they work with, they will see the politics melt away. For example, communicate the objectives of the account team and share those openly. Seek input from all members of the account team and acknowledge their contributions. Publish the proceedings and decisions from key account planning meetings. Communicate the benefits of working together to hit your goals as a team.

Show Leadership if You're in the Position; Otherwise, Don't Get Involved

If you are a leader within the sales organization, decide what type of culture you want and take actions to drive it. Culture has four major pressure points.

1. Culture starts with the message from leadership. Too many organizations communicate a message from leadership like "we're a collaborative organization" or "we're innovators" that receives little follow-through.

2. Culture is driven by what the organization practices and demonstrates. If you want a collaborative culture, leaders and teams within the organization have to demonstrate those behaviors. If those behaviors are new to the organization, demonstrating them allows others to watch and emulate those behaviors.

3. Culture is driven by what you measure and reward. If collaboration is important to the culture, find ways to measure it and then reward or recognize people for demonstrating those cultural attributes.

4. Culture is driven by courage. The leader has to have the courage to push the organization toward its cultural goals. She also has to have the courage to act and remove detractors from the culture. Sometimes this has to be done visibly to the organization to demonstrate the culture's importance.

If you're not a leader, don't try to extend your authority beyond its limits. While it might be tempting to step up and fill the silence left by a sales leader with his head in the sand, chances are you'll create additional conflict.

While my team and I eventually established an account planning process at the aforementioned technology services company, the political culture made the process longer and more complex. We watched the sales organization lose opportunities, we watched talented salespeople leave for healthier environments, and eventually we saw the CEO get fired. Politics do no favors for anyone. While bad behavior may seem tempting in the near term, I've never seen positive long-term results. Steer clear of political people, respect the priorities of others within your company, and keep what's best for your account at the center of your account plan.

5 Questions to Ask About Understanding the Politics

1. What role does leadership in your organization play in setting the cultural direction, and how can you support that?

2. Have you defined clear roles and responsibilities for the account planing process?

3. How is political behavior being addressed in your organization by leadership and by team members?

4. If you're a leader, how can you move more decisively to address your culture and politics?

5. How can you collaborate with your peers to address political challenges by identifying abundance, taking control, communicating, and leading?

Chapter 6

Think Big

A few months ago, my wife and I took our teenage daughters to Iceland. It was an incredible place, like an outdoor museum of geology, meteorology, and mythology with mountains, waterfalls, and extreme weather.

One day, we were driving along the southern coast to a well-known glacial waterfall, Skógafoss. It was easy to see as we approached—it's one of the largest waterfalls in Iceland, standing 200 feet high and 82 feet across with glacier fields in the distance behind it. We parked, and along with hundreds of other tourists, began walking closer.

The scene was truly magnificent. And yet, we knew the view was even better from the top. Most of the visitors just observe from the bottom of the waterfall, but there's a footpath that winds up the side of the mountain in a wide slalom, allowing almost anyone to meander up and enjoy the view from above. Being Donnolos, however, we were sure we could get there faster by skipping the path and scrambling straight up the side. So, with nothing more than our hands and determination, we started climbing.

It was an almost vertical trek. As we climbed, volcanic rock rolled loose beneath our hands and feet and tumbled down the mountain. I began to realize this was slightly dangerous and probably crazy. But we persevered. We knew we could get there because we had seen other people do it, and we knew it was better than the sight from the bottom because we had seen pictures, even though 90 percent of the tourists seemed satisfied with the view from below. A few were taking pictures of us.

We were rewarded at the top. The view was spectacular in every direction. Literally as far as the eye can see—which on this day was about 20 miles because we could make out the famous rock formations along the coast in Dyrhólaey. Behind us rose the massive Mýrdalsjökull glacier. The waterfall itself was more impressive from above, roaring with power that couldn't be appreciated the same way from below. We could see the water flowing beneath us away from the falls, marking its path across the stark volcanic rock and on to the northern Atlantic Ocean.

Despite the arduous climb, we were pretty happy at the top.

Mountain climbs like this are an easy analogy to achieving any goal. Both require an objective, sometimes beyond what you think you can accomplish. They produce challenges along the way. Aspirational account plans require the strength and commitment of mountain climbing, but they need something else as well. To reach the goals set by an aspirational account plan, you have to know what the view looks like from the top. You have to be able to visualize how you got there—not just the continued journey up, but the leaps, shortcuts, and dodged falling rock. You have to think big—to want to climb the mountain, rather than be satisfied with the view below or to take the slow, meandering path up. That direct, vertical hike offers achievement beyond what you might have accomplished otherwise.

Aspirational account plans are unique. Almost every company will have strategic account plans (determined by the 20 percent of accounts that generate 80 percent of the revenue); they will have tactical plans for their transactional products and services; and they will most likely have pursuit plans that focus on winning new business. In my experience, few companies devote additional time to aspirational plans. While it may not be an idea you've considered before, aspirational account plans can apply to the sales organization in any company.

In this chapter, I'll cite examples from large business-to-business companies with aspirational revenue amounts in the $50 million to $100 million range, because that number is significantly larger than their average deal size of $2 million. If your average deal size is $100,000, your aspirational revenue numbers might be in the $1 million to $2 million range. The point of aspirational account planning is to step out of the comfort zone of incremental thinking (growing the account 10 percent by next year, for example) and believe that you can climb straight up the mountain. While incremental thinking has a place in strategic and tactical account plans, aspirational account plans require much bigger steps and innovative thinking.

Thinking Big Requires Vision

Last year, my team and I worked on three aspirational account plans with Glenn Hoogerwerf, president of the software business unit for Aricent, a product engineering services firm. Hoogerwerf asked three of his superstar sales teams to create an account plan that would get their customer to $100 million in the next three to five years. For each of those accounts, $100 million was an enormous leap from the current revenue, and it took the sales teams weeks to adjust to what Hoogerwerf was asking. So Hoogerwerf had to change their perspective. He asked them to imagine they were five years in the future, and they had already achieved the $100 million account goal. He then asked them to describe what that account looked like, in terms of Aricent resources. How many new salespeople were working on that account team? What were their roles? Although part of the Aricent sales team, did they physically work at the customer's offices so they could be an on-site resource? Which customer departments were using Aricent's services? What changes had been made to Aricent's delivery systems?

"I always try to work backwards from the end goal," says Hoogerwerf. "What will the account look like five years from now when we're a $100 million account? It's easier for people to describe the end state of what the operational footprint would look like—where the business would be coming from, specifically which division, which services—at that end state. Once you can describe it at the end state, work backwards to your next milestone. What does it look like four years from now? Three? Then work backwards to one year from now; then work backwards to today."

Once the sales team can begin to describe the end state, Hoogerwerf asks them to describe each year leading up to that. If year five is $100 million with 20 new Aricent employees and a new delivery center closer to the customer, how much of that has been done by year four? By year three? Hoogerwerf asks his team to map out the steps, year by year, necessary to complete that five-year vision.

"You have a vision that you're articulating to people: 'Here's where our business is going to go, here's what we're going to try to achieve. I want to be the number one vendor, I want to be the number one product, I want to have this number of licenses.' You can now very quickly articulate where you're going, what your vision is," he explains.

You should be able to articulate where the revenue will come from and how much will come from each division. Then you can start thinking operationally about how to make that happen. What kind of sales team will you need? What kind of marketing will you need? What kind of products will you need to bring to the table? What engineering or operational team do you need to bring in? Those are the mechanisms of how you're going to do it.

Thinking Big Goes Beyond Increments

While strategic, tactical, and pursuit plans rely on incremental growth, incremental goals don't work for aspirational account plans. Growing a $1 million account by 10 percent for five years will get you to about $1.6 million. But consider what might happen if that same customer is deemed an aspirational account, and the goal is set at $25 million. Your thinking understandably changes, and chances are even if you achieve only half of that $25 million in five years, the account will be far more successful and valuable to your company than if you had limited it to annual incremental growth.

It's worth noting the obvious here: Not every account qualifies as a potential aspirational account. I'm talking about Fortune 500 companies that can spend tens of millions of dollars on individual vendors and partners. And as part of your aspirational account plan you have to ensure that you can deliver your product or service at that level, within the timeframe you've set out. You'll likely have to invest heavily in your own company or acquire another company to meet the demands, but that's all part of the plan.

Once you've identified an aspirational account, here are some pitfalls to avoid so you don't lapse into incremental account planning:

- **Incremental account planning gives your competitors an advantage.** You should have a goal regarding your competitors in your aspirational account plan. Do you want to be one of 100 vendors for your client? Do you want to be in the top 10? Is your goal to be one of their top three partners? With incremental thinking, you can never answer that question, because you're not looking at the long-term competitive landscape. You're looking to win incremental business in a few short-term areas. Aspirational planning charts a path to differentiate yourself this year, become a core partner next year, and be a top 10 provider in year three.

- **Incremental account planning promotes short-term thinking rather than a long-term strategy.** For example, imagine you're not hitting your account plan goals in Q2 and the team is behind in its quota. Incremental thinking says, "I'll cut back on my costs because the revenue isn't there." Ironically, cutting costs at this point sacrifices any long-term investment for short-term returns. If you don't have an account plan that says, "Here's where I need to be year one, here's where I need to be year two, here's where I need to be year three," in terms of resources, relationships, and strategic goals, you don't have a framework for judging those investments. Instead of investing in a $100 million partnership, all you're really doing is incremental, tactical transactions. You won't ever make a strategic move because you'll gauge any investment on short-term results. It can be very misleading, and there's a danger of reconsidering your entire strategy because you missed that near-term mark. Sometimes you have to have perseverance that says, "I'm going to continue to invest, because I need to get to this specific point in the future."

- **Short-term wins can take you down the wrong path.** We've all been in a scenario where a surprise win catches our attention. It becomes the shiny object that we want to chase, thinking that this win surely marks a road full of many similar wins. Unfortunately, it might be an area that isn't going to yield a lot of long-term business. While it might seem attractive today—your team is beating its numbers and you're getting great revenue—it might burn out quickly. You risk diverting investment into an area that has limited long-term potential because you had a positive short-term experience.

Think about setting a destination in your GPS. You have a goal: a point B that you want to get to from your point A. There might be traffic on one street, and your GPS will reroute you to another street. But the end destination is always in mind, right? When it comes to aspirational account planning, you must keep the end destination in mind.

Motivation and Challenges

The concept of long-term aspirational planning is not easy to grasp. Even in Hoogerwerf's case, when presenting the challenge to his sales teams, they were used to incremental thinking. Sitting in a small conference room in San Francisco, we heard comments like, "This will take 10-15 years," and, "The customer will never let us have proportionately that much business," and, "We're too small," from the first team. The other two teams reacted similarly. Hoogerwerf wasn't concerned with his teams' ability to get to $100 million with these accounts, but with their perceptions that they couldn't.

One reason the teams were apprehensive about a $100 million account was that they linked it to their quota attainment. There were about three salespeople on each account team, and it didn't take long to calculate how much revenue each would be responsible for toward this goal. And since their sales compensation was tied to quota attainment, they quickly became concerned about cutting into their own wallets.

The terms *goal* and *quota* are often used synonymously, but there is an important distinction when designing aspirational account plans. Focusing too much on quota can limit a sales representative's thinking because it affects his near-term commitments—and his compensation. It's hard for sales team members to talk about how they're going to build their quota because they naturally want to minimize anything being added to it. They fear that their next quota will be unattainable, and they will thus earn less money. Or, that they might attain that quota and be punished the following year with an even higher one.

But goals and quotas are not the same. Quota conversations start with, "What am I going to sell next year and how much will that affect my compensation?" Aspirational goal conversations start with, "Where am I going to be five years from now with this account?" These plans focus on the long-term objectives, and ask salespeople to disconnect the aspirational goal from what their quota will be for next year. Figure 6-1 illustrates how an aspirational perspective can propel you beyond any quota barriers.

Figure 6-1. Goal vs. Quota

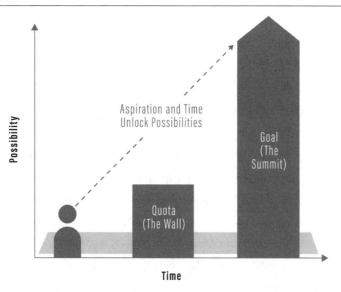

In aspirational account plans, the sales team has to think beyond its quota. Setting a revenue goal for the account and a deadline to achieve that goal helps salespeople overcome the imaginary "wall" created by their quota.

When my family and I were climbing the Skógafoss in Iceland, we knew we could get to the top because we could see other people ahead of us who had done it, even those crazy enough to climb straight up. The same is true when motivating your team to achieve their goals in an aspirational account. Look at companies that are already doing $50 million or $100 million with a particular customer. What are they doing? What value are they offering? How are they working with the account? What's the difference between what you're doing and what that competitor is doing? How can you look like that or look even better than that?

For example, my company, SalesGlobe, provides consulting services to clients. If we can't see our way to a bigger number—a multiple number—with an account we've identified as an aspirational account, then we might look at what another large consulting firm is doing with that account in terms of the value they provide, how they work with the client, and their level of financial engagement. Or, we might look at what other consulting firms are doing with accounts similar to our client. This shows us what can be done and often done better to provide greater value to the client. In the same way, think about what your team could provide to an account. You might see yourself in a frame that's too small. But if a similar company is generating $50 million of revenue with that account—perhaps even one of your competitors—then it stands to reason that you can too.

In my experience, there are three reasons why a company cannot accomplish a $100 million account: opportunity, timeframe, and capability.

Opportunity

Opportunity is the ability for the customer to buy or consume your product or service. If a company similar to yours is doing $70 million of business with an account, that may be an addressable opportunity. If the customer is already purchasing at that level, the opportunity is there. If one of the customer's competitors or another company in a similar industry is consuming $70 million of a product or service similar to yours, the opportunity is there.

If a customer is not used to buying at that level, this could be a latent opportunity. Consider how you can help the customer find new markets or increase the demand for your services.

Timeframe

How fast can all of this be enabled? If the opportunity is there, then the next step is to set a timeframe and start with a hypothesis: "We think three years is enough time for us to get to this level with our customer." Once you set a timeframe and a revenue goal, you have a trajectory for the aspirational account value (Figure 6-2). You know how fast the sales team will have to work over a certain period of years. A goal set with a deadline starts the action.

Figure 6-2. Goal Plus Time Equals Trajectory

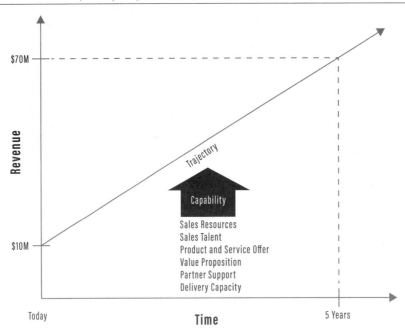

Setting a revenue goal and a deadline to achieve it creates a trajectory that defines a path to achievement. In the example above, the aspirational goal for the account is $70 million in five years. During that five years, the sales team will have to make decisions about its ability to service a $70 million account. Working with other internal functions, the company may have to increase its capabilities. Specifically, this means hiring additional sales resources, training or coaching salespeople to increase sales talent, expanding product and service offers, differentiating value proposition, adding partner support, and increasing delivery capacity.

Capability

Capability refers to resources, talent, and funding. Once the trajectory has been set, look backward and see what you need in terms of sales resources, sales talent, product or service offers, the value proposition, and partner support for access or delivery. You'll have certain requirements for each of these areas that are included in the account plan. While it may not be fair to get saddled with a significantly bigger goal each year with the same resources, it's perfectly fair and reasonable to take on a big, aspirational goal for an account with the condition that certain capability be provided by the company.

Another important key to goal attainment is emotion. The sales team members need to want to reach this aspirational goal; they're probably going to need a little extra oxygen for the climb. So help them visualize their personal perspective. What will it look like for the sales team when they're at $70 million? Perhaps they'll sell across all of your lines of business. They'll be working at a different level of the customer's company, with the president and the COO. They'll be spending a lot of time at their New York headquarters. They'll be talking about bigger ideas and partnering with major companies that complement your offer, having strategic conversations. The team has to know what it would look like from their eyes and feel like to live it. It's not just a P&L exercise. It has to be visual, tangible, and exciting to the team.

Getting Your Customer Involved

An account plan is all about the customer, but a lot of companies write their plans without any customer input. They're planning for the account rather than with the account. You may be able to get away with it for tactical account plans, but strategic accounts will suffer without customer involvement. And you'll never reach an aspirational goal without the customer. You can't grow an aspirational account by climbing every rung of the ladder by yourself—it will take you decades. You have to jump rungs and take leaps, and you need the customer's help.

My team and I recently told one of our clients, Scott, about our intention to become a strategic partner and substantially increase our revenue with his company. His initial reaction was surprise because we're not doing anything like that now. He considered it for a minute, and the idea of becoming strategic partners began to take shape. He said, "OK, you will have to hire a team internally to be able to manage the technical aspects of this." He saw the opportunity and benefit to his business over that timeframe. Then he started talking about capability. He started telling us what we needed to do differently to meet that threshold. He started to talk about the technological requirements. Scott started to see the possibilities.

Once he started to think about us differently he realized the opportunities for him and his company. His tone changed, and he began to think of ways he could help us get there. He went very quickly from disbelief to wanting to enable us.

"Taking this idea to your client is important, because it raises your visibility to them," says Hoogerwerf. You might not even be on the customer's radar screen; however, by saying that you want to do $100 million of business within three years, and having a plan to get there, suddenly the customer will start thinking about you differently, rather than as just another supplier.

"One of our largest customers has 1,000 vendors," Hoogerwerf says. "They get peppered every single day by somebody asking them for business. Do you want to be one of the thousand, or do you want to be a strategic partner? You have to communicate that in your first sentence."

Aspirational accounts are built around a 360-degree relationship with the customer. That relationship must include:

- **What you can sell to the customer.** This includes all the core components of the account plan with a few key differences. First, the objective is a lot bigger—a lot more aspirational. Second, you're usually selling higher up in the organization to more senior-level buyers. Third, your value proposition has to be a lot more meaningful, clear, and connected to financial return for the client. Fourth, you are usually partnering more creatively with other complementary organizations that can give you better access to senior levels, strengthen your offer and value proposition, and enable you to deliver on a larger scale.

- **How you can help that customer sell more.** How can you help the customer increase its growth as a partner, through different ways to market? Where are the synergies between your businesses? This is where you ask, "How do we do something that we haven't already done? How do we do something that we haven't thought of?" That's the magic point, and where the fun begins.

- **What you can buy from the customer.** It might not always be possible to purchase the products or services of your customer, but it's worth looking for reciprocity points.

Think about the aspirational revenue amount—let's say $100 million—as 360 degrees of total value. A certain percent is what you sell, a certain percent is what you help the customer sell, and a certain percent is what you buy. The $100 million may not be pure revenue to your company; you might sell $80 million to the customer, help it go to market for a total of $18 million, and purchase $2 million of its products or services. Or the balance may be different depending on the opportunities.

When we first began working with Aricent on its aspirational account plans, Hoogerwerf set three goals: Become a $100 million account, accomplish that within three years, and create a 360-degree relationship.

"For some of our major customers, $100 million is the minimum threshold for attention as a partner or as a vendor," says Hoogerwerf. "It's a critical mass number to them. That's what it takes to be a strategic player. For another account, maybe that threshold is $1 billion; for another account, it may be $10 million.

"The 360-degree relationship says not only do we want to sell our products to them, but we would like to buy their products and we want to help them go to market with their products," he continues. "If you only sell to these aspirational accounts, as opposed to purchase from them, you're a tactical player; you're not a strategic partner. The 360-degree relationship is a qualifier to being a strategic partner."

Aspirational plans consider the coverage model in a different way, too, says Hoogerwerf. "We want to sell across all divisions, not just take that one division and work that neighborhood, but work across the entire company. There also has to be a timeframe, like three years, that creates a trajectory. Every conversation I have with the client, I use that. I'll say, 'Hey, our goal is to be a $100 million, 360-degree partner across all your product divisions.' And then I can start articulating how we're going to help them. It should be simple and succinct. 'I'm growing it to $100 million, and I'm going to do that by having key relationships with three to five $20 million accounts, and then some medium-size businesses in these three markets of software, Internet services, and media and entertainment.'

"They might ask me how I'm going to do it, but that's what a great account plan should do; it should draw you in. It should tell a compelling story of how you're going to get there, and what it's going to look like when it comes together.

"Forget what you have to achieve in the next quarter. Thinking three years out is easier and tends to break inhibitions. It shows a lot of ideas and potential. A good account plan should point to the areas of opportunity and come up with ideas that can be explored," he concludes.

It pays to think big and plan big. To start, you may identify a few of your accounts that warrant the time and investment of an aspirational account plan. Your goal should be big enough to shock you and your team at first, but it should be somewhere in the realm of imaginable after more thought. Start with the accounts that represent sizeable opportunities, set an aspirational goal and timeframe, get your team's head into the mindset of what it looks and feels like in the future to be at that level, and then work back to how you got there with the capabilities and short-term goals you need to achieve over your timeframe.

5 Questions to Ask About Thinking Big

1. What handful of accounts might warrant aspirational account plans?
2. What aspirational goals and timeframes are in the realm of possibility?
3. What does it look like when you reach that goal in terms of who is on your team, what it's doing differently, and the value it's offering the client?
4. How have you engaged your customer in a conversation about your aspiration with a tangible number?
5. How will you work with your customer to get there?

Conclusion

Advice From Experts

Throughout *Essential Account Planning,* we've looked at account planning in terms of how it fits within the context of the business, how each component functions, and how the many different teams within a company can facilitate the creation of an essential account plan. Use this book as a starting point as you begin your account planning process. It will provide you with the priorities and structures you can use to frame your approach. Refer to this book as a field guide as you work through the process with your team. Reflect upon the examples and stories about how other organizations conduct their planning to give your team ideas. The appendix has templates you can use directly for your plans. Feel free to modify them to meet your needs. Your approach should be based on the requirements of your business and your clients.

Now it's time to assess the effectiveness of your current account plans and processes. I've included an account planning report card in appendix 13; take the assessment to learn about your current account planning processes and where you can improve. Grade your organization according to the description that best matches your performance in each area. You can use the Essential Account Planning Report Card with your team to get consensus on where you stand and where you'll want to focus to improve, so you can dramatically increase results with your biggest, most important accounts.

Let me know your results at mark.donnolo@salesglobe.com, or on Twitter @MarkDonnolo #EssentialAccountPlanning.

Finally, here is some essential account planning advice from sales leaders who have taken the lessons in this book to heart.

Happy (well-planned) selling!

Commitment

Brad Kaegi, Senior Director of Marketing, Merial: "Maintain the commitment. As priorities come along and events happen in your marketplace, your willingness to continue on with the process can diminish. Or certain events can cause you to walk away. But, I think the magic has been our ability to not only improve the process, but also continue to execute it—not allowing other events to distract us. We could easily say, 'Well, we're going to launch these new products, so we're going into launch mode and we're going to pause account planning.' Events can interrupt your process, but you have to be committed and make sure it's maintained."

Camie Shelmire, Chief Client Officer, Aricent: "Make it manageable, especially in the beginning. Make the actions simple and actionable. Make sure you have someone responsible for bringing the team together and reviewing for accountability, and have a senior executive hold them accountable. Stage one is making the team accountable. Stage two is seeing the improvements in growth."

Sue Holub, Vice President of Enterprise Software Marketing, Lexmark International: "Start with understanding what you want to achieve by going down that path of account planning at all. Commit to it at the most senior levels. Like any other change in an organization, there will be significant resistance to behavioral change, especially among salespeople. It's as much of a culture change as a process and discipline change. And so, if you go into it halfhearted, that's exactly what you'll get out of it."

Participation

David Long, Vice President of Strategic Sales, LexisNexis: "Devote the time to make the account planning process the best that it can possibly be, and ensure an acceptable level of participation from all the partnering organizations. We've got a good process in place; we have a very actionable process in place. But again, it's only as good as the engagement."

Robert Dillon, Managing Director, Americas Agency Development, Google: "Set a clear expectation. Make the teams have something at risk. Have in-person reviews. It's an opportunity to see if it's working the way we want and for us to celebrate success. Get involved personally. We pull in operating groups of six at a time on the team. I sample the executive summits to see how the conversations are happening with the client once a quarter. And for us, there is long-term compensation at risk in their incentive plans as well."

Mike Barnes, Executive Vice President, Andrews Distributing: "Enroll your entire team in the account planning process. It's important to involve your operating team, your brand team, your commercial marketing, marketing services, and all the support teams that serve your sales team as a customer. The sales team has to be the customer of these teams. Make sure that anybody that's involved in the operations understands how they affect each other. Share the plan, but also share the post-evaluation."

Scott Taylor, Director of Global Sales Operations and Worldwide Sales, Inter-Continental Hotels Group: "Align everyone—all the different parts of the organization that are involved in sales and sales enablement—with what you're trying to accomplish. When we have taken the time to fully socialize our goals and objectives as an organization, and everyone shares the same vision, that's when we're successful. When everyone doesn't have a clear understanding of what that vision is, but they have their interpretation of it, and they're working very hard to execute their interpretation, that's when we have not been as successful. Having a clear, well-defined, well-communicated company-wide strategy is what has led us to be successful with account planning."

Ownership

John Dupree, Partner, Opus Faveo Innovation Development; Former Senior Vice President of Business Sales, Sprint: "If it's not important to you, don't pretend it's important to your team, because it won't be. And it ruins your credibility. Don't harp about account planning, and then never ask about it or use it yourself. If account planning is important to you, find a few ways to reinforce its significance during the year. If you go to see two or three accounts with your team and you haven't asked for an account plan or accessed it in your CRM, they're pretty certain that you're not that interested in it."

Jill Merken, Vice President of Global Sales Operations and Inside Sales, SafeNet: "Believe in the account plan, inspect it, and use it. If you don't, don't ask people to do it. Find the medium that you want, whether it's 20 pages or two pages. Then, hold everyone accountable to do it. Otherwise, don't bother, because you won't be successful. And that's what I think most companies do; they start, and stop, the process. Leaders who use account planning value it a lot. Once it's in place, account planning should not be an option."

Buy-In

Cillian O'Grady, Corporate Sales, SMB EMEA Sales Leader, Citrix GetGo: "Companies get this notion that everybody is going to do account planning, and they invest so much in training, and then they mandate it. And people don't really have the buy-in. They start seeing it as a chore and administrative work. You get better results, and people are more likely to adopt a process if they see other people being successful with it. Whereas, if your colleague asks, 'How did you grow this account from $12 million to $50 million over two years?' and the answer is, 'Well, it started with the company account plan.' That's a very powerful story."

Deborah Wudel, Director of Sales Operations, CSC: "From a sales enablement point of view, it's clarity of communications around why you're doing it. Sales-people don't want to do this. It's a heck of a lot of time and effort. It's a lot of formalizing information that's maybe in someone's head, but they're thinking, 'What's in it for me?' You have to articulate that a particular form of an account plan, length of an account plan, and the process itself has really led to wins that would otherwise have been left undiscovered. You need to be able to put that argument together. And what I've found in many of the account plans is that it was the conversation that was most important; it was the discussion, the meeting people, the building the team—not the document—that ended up being important.

Appendix 1

Competitive Landscape

These charts help you understand your position in the market and where you may need to strengthen your position or be aware of intense competition. The chart in the back lists your direct competitors for this account, their value proposition (what each competitor can specifically offer the customer, such as lowest pricing or broadest range of services), and the strengths and weaknesses of each competitor for that specific account. You can also rank competitors from strongest to weakest by offer, as illustrated in the front chart.

Competitor	Value Proposition: What They Offer the Account	Strengths	Vulnerabilities
Allied Industries	• We offer global capabilities and resources that allow us to partner with you to operationalize your strategy.	• A broad set of offerings. • Expertise in the customer's industry. • Global scale.	• Seen as large and slow to respond. • Generalists rather than experts.

Competitor	Rank	Offer 1	Offer 2	Offer 3	Offer 4
Consolidated	1	Allied Industries	Radial Inc.	TSE	Federated Company
	2	Consolidated	Allied Industries	Radial Inc.	Taggart Transco
Federated Company	3	Federated Company	Federated Company	Consolidated	TSE
	4	TSE	Consolidated	Rand	Consolidated
Radial Inc.	5	Radial Inc.	Tech Partners	Federated Company	Rand
Taggart Transco					

Directions: In the first column, list your direct competitors for this account. In the proceeding columns, list the value proposition and the strengths and weaknesses of each competitor regarding this specific account.

Competitor	Value Proposition: What They Offer the Account	Strengths	Vulnerabilities

Directions: List your offers (products or services) across the top row. Then, in the columns beneath each offer, rank your competitors for each of those offers, from strongest to weakest. This chart helps you see your position with the customer against your competitors.

Rank				
1				
2				
3				
4				
5				

Appendix 2

Customer Challenges
and Priorities

A customer performance chart can tell you about the financial trend of the company and indicate whether the company is performing well or has challenges. Listing the challenges and priorities of the customer will also help you look for opportunities in which your products and services solve their challenges and align with their priorities.

Challenges	Priorities
• Has underperformed the NASDAQ by more than 25% over the last three years. • Mobile business continues to decline. • Services are a primary contributor to growth but are under threat. • Hardware markets remain under pressure.	• New mobile devices for new market segments. • Sourcing new technology development talent. • Making strategic acquisitions. • Converting operating expense to CAPX.

Directions: List the challenges and priorities of your customer.

Challenges	Priorities

SWOT Analysis

A traditional SWOT analysis, from the perspective of your sales organization, will help your team focus its efforts.

Strengths	Weaknesses
• We are a preferred supplier. • Good penetration in the mobile business. • Products are well received. • Strong relationships in the divisions we are in.	• Cloud offerings need to be strengthened. • Haven't been able to quantify the ROI of our products. • Our aggressive pricing leaves little profit for investment.

Opportunities	Threats
• Good inroads into new business units. • Successes with our past work makes a good case for new business units. • Customer willing to co-invest in new initiatives with us.	• A large portion of our business comes through RFPs, which have price pressure. • Our increased presence has drawn attention from larger competitors in the account.

Directions: Complete the SWOT analysis by listing the strengths, weaknesses, opportunities, and threats of your sales organization regarding your account. Remember this SWOT analysis is from the perspective of your company: What are the strengths of your sales organization? What are the weaknesses of your sales organization?

Strengths	Weaknesses

Opportunities	Threats

Needs by Division

Listing the needs of the company helps uncover unknown opportunities.

Acme Overall	Division 1	Division 2	Division 3
1. Support of the company's innovation positioning.	1. Speed to market with the new mobile platform.	1. Improved network performance of big hardware products.	1. Determining whether services should be a profit center.
2. Need for more cloud-based services.	2. Responding to customer needs for improved product functionality.	2. Bundling hardware and services solutions.	2. Bundling services with hardware and mobile.
3. Increasing requirement to show ROI from technology investments.	3. Positioning for corporate investment vs. other divisions.	3. Responding to customer needs for hardware and mobile integration.	3. Improving the talent base of the services organization.

Directions: List the major needs of the customer company overall in the first column. Across the top row, list the names of divisions that are most likely to purchase your products and services. Then, below each of those divisions, list the specific needs of each of those divisions. Remember to list the needs from the customer's perspective.

Account Map and Team Alignments

These charts help identify whom you know at the customer company and whom you do not. The Account Map chart helps paint a clearer picture of your relationship with a client point of contact and how your sales team might provide solutions to that person. The Team Alignments chart maps executives at the customer company to people at your company. For example, if Paul Adams is the president of the customer company, you might need to pull in Charlie Cooper, the president of your company, to help build the relationship.

Account Map

Executive at Customer	Title	Organization or Division	Buying Decision Role	Relationship Strength	Frequency of Contact	What They Currently Buy	Annual Value of That Buy	What Else They Could Buy	Their Top Challenge
Paul Adams	President	Hardware Division	Financial Sponsor	Low	Serri Annually	Core Software Suite and Tech Services	$11,000,000	Full Suite and Professional Services	Cutting the cost of operations and converting to CAPX.
John James	EVP of Operations	Wireless Infrastructure	Decision Maker	Moderate	Quarterly	Core Software Suite	$2,500,000	Full Suite and Professional Services	Finding the biggest impact for R&D spend.
Walt Mansell	Director of Engineering	Wireless Infrastructure	Project Owner and Influencer	High	Monthly	Core Software Suite	$2,500,000	Full Suite and Professional Services	Flawless operational execution and meeting SLAs.

Team Alignments

Executive at Customer	Account Team Member	Role in Account	What Should This Account Team Member Do for Our Customer?	How Should This Account Team Member Work With Our Team?
Paul Adams	Charlie Cooper, President	Create the peer-to-peer executive relationship between our company and the customer.	Understand strategic priorities and position us.	Provide our team with strategic direction for our account plan.
John James	Warren Peacemaker, Account Leader	Customer relationship management. Handles strategic planning and goal attainment.	Lead the articulation of our value proposition.	Give the team guidance on our goals and hold the team accountable.
Walt Mansell	Sanjay Sharma, Sales Subject Matter Expert	Fulfill value proposition and identify additional opportunities to serve the customer.	Provide "white glove" customer experience for the customer.	Execute the account plan, collaborate with team for insight on customer priorities.

Directions: In the first column, list executives at the customer company, including buyers and influencers. Complete the information across the row for each. For Relationship Strength, write "High" if the person will easily take a meeting with you, "Moderate" if you've met them and they would likely take a meeting, and "Low" if you've met them but they might not take a meeting. Write "None" if you haven't met the person.

Account Map

Executive at Customer	Title	Organization or Division	Buying Decision Role	Relationship Strength	Frequency of Contact	What They Currently Buy	Annual Value of That Buy	What Else They Could Buy	Their Top Challenge

Directions: In the first column, list executives at the customer company from the Account Map. Complete the information across the row for each of the executives, mapping executives at the customer company to people at your company.

Team Alignments

Executive at Customer	Account Team Member	Role in Account	What Should This Account Team Member Do for Our Customer?	How Should This Account Team Member Work With Our Team?

Appendix 6

Offer White Space Map

The Offer White Space Map helps identify divisions in which you have specific opportunities and in which you might be missing opportunities.

Offers / Divisions	Product A	Product B	Product C	Product D	Product E
Division 1	$750,000	$851,700	WHITE SPACE	$1,395,000	$787,500
Division 2	$1,012,500	WHITE SPACE	$1,972,500	WHITE SPACE	WHITE SPACE
Division 3	$1,012,500	$240,000	$2,205,000	WHITE SPACE	WHITE SPACE
Division 4	$1,012,500	WHITE SPACE	WHITE SPACE	WHITE SPACE	$862,500
Division 5	WHITE SPACE	WHITE SPACE	$907,500	WHITE SPACE	$5,250,000

Directions: In the first column, list the divisions in the customer company that might purchase your products and services. Then, in the top row, list your products and services. Complete the matrix, assigning dollar values where specific divisions might purchase a specific product. White spaces indicate zero revenue or revenue below a certain threshold. These may be places where you don't have the right relationships or you may not have considered that product for that division in the past.

Offers Divisions					

Goal Build by Opportunity

The Goal Build chart helps you understand how you will achieve your quota or revenue goal with this account. It lists your revenue goal for this account, and then each opportunity and its value that will help you advance to that goal.

FY18 GOAL	
Revenue Goal	$43,000,000
Revenue Identified	$13,680,000
New Revenue Needed	**$29,320,000**
Multiple of New Revenue Target	2.5
Multiple of New Revenue Target ($)	$73,300,000

FY18 GOAL BUILD	
Opportunity	**Value**
Systems Infrastructure	$5,600,000
Partner Management Program	$3,400,000
Support Services	$9,000,000
Network Rollout Optimization	$12,500,000
Lab Management Outsourcing	$14,300,000
Allied Services Partnership	$8,500,000
APAC Assessment	$1,500,000
New Product Development Support	$13,700,000
Market Launch Readiness	$2,300,000
NewCo Acquisition Integration	$4,500,000
Systems Testing	$1,400,000
TOTAL	**$76,700,000**
Surplus (Deficit)	**$3,400,000**

Directions: In the top section, list your Revenue Goal (your financial goal for this account) and Revenue Identified (revenue coming in from prior sales or recurring revenue). Subtract the Revenue Identified from the Revenue Goal and list in the New Revenue Needed row. Next, select a multiple and put it in the Multiple of New Revenue Target row. (Best practices state that you should have between 2.5 and 3 times the revenue needed in your pipeline to meet your financial goals.) Multiply New Revenue Needed by your multiple, and put that number in the Multiple of New Revenue Target ($) row. In the bottom section, list opportunities within this account and their value. This exercise requires some thinking, but you should be able to identify enough opportunities to total to the Multiple of New Revenue Target. This number and the opportunities listed will become a critical focal point for your account plan.

GOAL	
Revenue Goal	
Revenue Identified	
New Revenue Needed	
Multiple of New Revenue Target	
Multiple of New Revenue Target ($)	

GOAL BUILD	
Opportunity	Value
TOTAL	
Surplus (Deficit)	

Strategy and Action Plan by Opportunity

The Strategy and Action Plan by Opportunity offers detail behind each known opportunity in the account, including the customer challenge your team is solving for the customer, your value proposition against competitors, and a high-level summary of the strategy to win this opportunity. The Strategy worksheet details each identified opportunity. The Action Plan describes specific near-term actions to advance the opportunity. This section should be reviewed regularly to ensure that the actions are completed and to update with new action items.

Strategy

Opportunity Name:	New Product Development Support
Opportunity Value:	$13,700,000

Customer's Top Challenge
Cutting the cost of operations and converting to CAPX.

Value Proposition
We are uniquely qualified to not only convert operating costs to CAPX but also address your go-to-market needs for new product development and implementation support.

Summary of Strategy
Strengthen customer senior executive relationships with our organization's senior executives. Provide insights with our research on cost conversion and rapid product innovation. Propose joint investment between our organizations in product development.

Action Plan

Specific Action	Description	Owner	Timing
Strenghten executive relationships.	Brief our COO, CTO, and CSO on the strategy and value proposition. Set customer connection schedule.	Warren Peacemaker Charlie Cooper, Sponsor	Briefings by 1/15 Connection schedule by 1/31
Customize research.	Leverage research on cost conversion to align the customer's industry challenges.	Sanjay Sharma Research Team	By 2/15
Create investment messages.	Develop investment strategy alternatives for the two organizations.	Warren Peacemaker Finance	By 2/28

Directions: Complete the Strategy section of the worksheet to see detail for each identified opportunity. In the Action Plan section, describe specific near-term actions that your team can use to advance the opportunity. Include the owner of each action and a specific timeline for completion.

Strategy

Opportunity Name:	
Opportunity Value:	

Customer's Top Challenge

Value Proposition

Summary of Strategy

Action Plan

Specific Action	Description	Owner	Timing

Team Commitments

The Team Commitments chart lists the help you need from within your own company. The Specific Action column lists an action carried over from the Action Plan (appendix 8).

Team Commitments		January		
Offers Divisions	**Owner**	**Commitment**	**Actual**	**Status**
Specific Action (From Action Plan)	Warren Peacemaker	Brief COO, CTO, CSO.	Set up meetings to discuss.	In Progress
Strengthen executive relationships.	Charlie Cooper	Introduce approach to executives.	Completed conversations.	Met
Strengthen executive relationships.	Sanjay Sharma	Determine customer customization needs.	Mark research reports for additional data cuts.	Met
Customize research.	Research Team	Customize reports for customer.	Sourcing additional data to modify results.	Pending

Directions: Continually review and update action items in this chart for effective account planning.

Team Commitments				
Offers Divisions	Owner	Commitment	Actual	Status

Appendix 10

Budget and Forecast

Together with the Action Plan and Team Commitment charts (appendices 8 and 9, respectively), a Budget and Forecast Update chart can be reliable dashboards. They help you see progress of individual action items and the success the team is having with the account.

	FY18 Q1		FY18 Q2		FY18 Q3		FY18 Q4		FY18 Total	
	Budget	Forecast	Budget	Forecast	Budget	Forecast	Budget	Forecast	Budget	Forecast
Bookings	$7.5	$7.0	$7.5	$7.5	$7.5	$8.0	$7.5	$7.5	$29.9	$30.0
Revenue	$5.2	$4.8	$5.2	$5.3	$5.2	$6.0	$5.2	$5.3	$20.9	$21.3
EBITDA	$2.2	$1.8	$2.2	$2.3	$2.2	$2.5	$2.2	$2.3	$9.0	$8.8
EBITDA %	$0.3	$0.3	$0.3	$0.3	$0.3	$0.3	$0.3	$0.3	$0.3	$0.3

	FY18 Q1		FY18 Q2		FY18 Q3		FY18 Q4		FY18 Total	
	Budget	Forecast	Budget	Forecast	Budget	Forecast	Budget	Forecast	Budget	Forecast
Bookings										
Revenue										
EBITDA										
EBITDA %										

Appendix 11

Pursuit Scoring Matrix

The Pursuit Scoring Matrix helps predict your ability to win new business, especially in competitive situations. The higher your score, the more likely you are to win business with that account. For low scores, take action to gain industry knowledge or subject matter expertise, or build relationships within that account.

Account	Industry Knowledge?	Subject Matter Expertise?	Multiple Buyer Relationships?	Segment Fit?	Differentiated?	Incumbent Competitor?	Score (1 Point per Positive Answer)
Allied	Yes. Telecom.	No. A new area for us.	Some. Know the buyer but not leadership.	Yes. Midcap company.	No. New area for us and not strong.	Competitor works with another buyer in the account.	3
Mercury Industries	No. Industrial Manufacturing.	Yes. Numerous examples for references.	Yes. Have been growing relationship for 3 years.	Yes. Midcap company.	Yes. Strong subject matter expertise.	Haven't worked with a competitor for several years.	5

Directions: List each potential new customer in the first column, Account, and complete the corresponding information. Give yourself one point for each yes, and total in the final column.

Account	Industry Knowledge?	Subject Matter Expertise?	Multiple Buyer Relationships?	Segment Fit?	Differentiated?	Incumbent Competitor?	Score (1 Point per Positive Answer)

Appendix 12

Sources of Growth Calculation

This chart helps you understand what percent of revenue in your account is retained or churned from year to year. Additionally, you can determine whether new revenue comes from upselling or cross-selling in your current lines of business, or whether you need to find additional buyers (new acquisition revenue) within your customer to meet your revenue goal.

Account	Year 1 Revenue	Year 2 Revenue	Retained Revenue	Retained Revenue Rate	Upsell and Cross-Sell Revenue	Upsell and Cross Sell Revenue Rate	New Acquisition Revenue	New Acquisition Revenue Rate	Total Growth
Acme Services	$100	$110	$100	100%	$10	10%	$0	0%	10%
Advanced Tech	$100	$90	$90	90%	$0	0%	$0	0%	-10%
Allied Manufacturing	$0	$35	$0	0%	$0	0%	$35	100%	100%
American Central	$140	$70	$70	50%	$0	0%	$0	0%	-50%
Andover Holdings	$0	$10	$0	0%	$0	0%	$10	100%	100%
Applied Software	$120	$200	$120	100%	$80	67%	$0	0%	67%
Total	$460	$515	$380	83%	$90	20%	$45	10%	12%

Directions: Use this chart to determine the percentage of revenue you retain or churn, along with revenue gained from upselling or cross-selling, and if you need additional buyers.

Account	Year 1 Revenue	Year 2 Revenue	Retained Revenue	Retained Revenue Rate	Upsell and Cross-Sell Revenue	Upsell and Cross Sell Revenue Rate	New Acquisition Revenue	New Acquisition Revenue Rate	Total Growth
Acme Services	$100	$110	$100	100%	$10	10%	$0	0%	10%
Advanced Tech	$100	$90	$90	90%	$0	0%	$0	0%	-10%
Allied Manufacturing	$0	$35	$0	0%	$0	0%	$35	100%	100%
American Central	$140	$70	$70	50%	$0	0%	$0	0%	-50%
Andover Holdings	$0	$10	$0	0%	$0	0%	$10	100%	100%
Applied Software	$120	$200	$120	100%	$80	67%	$0	0%	67%
Total	$460	$515	$380	83%	$90	20%	$45	10%	12%

Essential Account Planning Report Card

Key 1: Use the Right Structure	
Grading Areas: Rate on a Scale of 10 (1: strongly disagree; 10: strongly agree)	
1. We have a clearly articulated vision for how the account plans and processes will work.	
2. The account plans all align with the sales strategy and comprise a piece of the goal.	
3. We have a well-defined account plan structure that is used consistently.	
Total for This Key	
Average Score for This Key (divide by 3)	

Key 2: Set the Goal	
Grading Areas: Rate on a Scale of 10 (1: strongly disagree; 10: strongly agree)	
1. We set goals for our accounts that are aggressive but achievable.	
2. Our goals consider intelligence and insight from our account plans.	
3. We consistently identify a multiple of the account goal (e.g., 2.5x) in potential opportunities from the account plan.	
Total for This Key	
Average Score for This Key (divide by 3)	

Key 3: Create the Habits	
Grading Areas: Rate on a Scale of 10 (1: strongly disagree; 10: strongly agree)	
1. Our account plans and process are simple and straightforward rather than overengineered.	
2. We have a living account planning process that operates according to a schedule throughout the year.	
3. Our team is accountable for plans and we effectively manage noncompliance.	
Total for This Key	
Average Score for This Key (divide by 3)	

Key 4: Understand the Politics	
Grading Areas: Rate on a Scale of 10 (1: strongly disagree; 10: strongly agree)	
1. Our leadership creates a healthy direction for our culture and sets good examples that minimize politics.	
2. We have established clear roles and ownership for the account planning process.	
3. If there are disagreements or differences, we find ways to come to agreement for the good of the organization.	
Total for This Key	
Average Score for This Key (divide by 3)	

Key 5: Think Big	
Grading Areas: Rate on a Scale of 10 (1: strongly disagree; 10: strongly agree)	
1. We set aspirational goals for select accounts that make us uncomfortable but excited.	
2. We have visualized as a team what it will look like professionally and personally when we reach that level.	
3. We engage our customers in our aspirational account planning.	
Total for This Key	
Average Score for This Key (divide by 3)	

Overall Results			
1. Use the Right Structure			
2. Set the Goal			
3. Create the Habits			
4. Understand the Politics			
5. Think Big			
Total			

Letter Grade Scale	
9-10	A: Great. You may be demonstrating a best practice.
8	B: Good. Determine how you can improve your lowest areas.
7	C: Risky. Create an action plan to improve as soon as you can.
6	D: Scraping Bottom. Fix this area immediately.
<6	F: Yikes! Stop the damage and question what you're doing.

Acknowledgments

This book goes far beyond me in terms of what it took to make it happen. Without the team at SalesGlobe, *Essential Account Planning* would not be possible. First among them is Collette Parker, our content leader, editor, and writer extraordinaire. Collette helped me take a subject that has many moving parts and get the message across clearly. She is dedicated to the SalesGlobe vision of helping sales leaders think about challenging topics in new ways, and she helps achieve that vision through the content we develop. Thank you, Collette, for your excellence, your wit, and your friendship.

Without great client work, we would have nothing to write about. Carrie Ward, Michelle Seger, Jim Benard, and Rebecca Sandberg have been at the core of the hard work and contributors to the thinking that helps our clients and their businesses. Thank you for being champions of excellence.

My wife, Blythe, has given me balance and reality. She inspires me while reminding me of what's really important when I drift into my frequent delusion that life is business. Through all of the travails, she has been at my side. Thank you, Blythe. My two talented daughters, Isabel and Olivia, continue to give me purpose for the long run. I am repeatedly amazed at how these two ladies have grown and how their talent will take them further than we expect. My parents, Paul and Christina Donnolo, gave me a real example of how anything is possible with the right vision, accountability, and work ethic. Their kid turned out to not be a lazy bum as they had feared, and I'm grateful that they are here to cheer me on. I can never thank them enough.

Thanks for reading this book. As an old author friend once joked about a great book he wrote, "It's one of those books that once you put it down, you just can't pick it up." I hope this book gave you some great ideas and a few good laughs. In the end, sales should be fun.

About the Author

Mark Donnolo is managing partner of SalesGlobe, a leading sales innovation firm. He is author of the books *The Innovative Sale, What Your CEO Needs to Know About Sales Compensation,* and *Essential Account Planning.* Mark has worked with Fortune 1000 companies around the world for the past 25 years, focusing on sales innovation, sales strategy, sales coverage, and sales motivation. He holds an MBA from the University of North Carolina at Chapel Hill and a BFA from the University of the Arts in Philadelphia. He has served on the Board of Trustees for the University of the Arts and serves on the Alumni Council for Kenan-Flagler Business School. Mark lives in Atlanta with his wife and daughters. When he's not consulting, writing, or spending time with his family, he enjoys driving through the woods in his Gator with his dog, Winston-Bubba.

Index

In this index, *f* denotes figure.